Choosing

Light-Heartedness

"You are a beautiful, incredible human being!
No matter how badly you have been hurt,
or how severely you have hurt other people,
it's never too late to change!
You always have the opportunity, at any moment,
to completely change the direction of your life!"

Choosing
Light-Heartedness

A 33-Day Journey to Overcome Anxiety,
Depression and Dysfunctional Family Issues

By Kari Joys MS

Dedication

I lovingly dedicate this book to my dear, sweet Mother,
for living her spirituality and role-modeling compassion daily;
And to my life-long friend Kathy Buchenauer,
for being my true, compassionate, lighthearted friend
and helping me heal emotionally and spiritually;
And to my spiritual mentors Ione Jenson and Alma Rose,
and all my magical, supportive friends, including
Raleigh Mikkelsen, Samuel Mahaffy, Staci Wright, Pete Hoslett,
Rikki Nichols, LeRoy Malouf, Judith Moralis, Angela Moore,
Lori Bruckman-Fiske, Dick and Donna Gilson, Shabir Bhat,
Nita Magnussan, Livina Hiacinth, Grant Kynaston,
Renee Rindernecht, Cathy Fleetwood, Deborah Warner and
Marta Shollenberger, and many other precious, wonderful souls,
for laughing and crying with me
and continuing to reach for the stars,
even at times when we're stuck in the mud;
And to my loving husband, John Fryling,
for being my loyal partner and computer expert
amidst the happy chaos of clients, workshops, family and writing;
And to my lovely nieces, Laure Larsen and Rhoda Joy Starks,
for remembering the 'fun' in *dysfunctional;*
And to my beautiful daughters,
Danielle Quade and Alexandra Witherwax,
for being so very charming, confident and successful
and surpassing anything I could have ever done at their young age;
And to my sweet, wise, adorable grandson, Malachi,
for being the light and joy of my life
and choosing lightheartedness every day;
To Princess Diana, for role-modeling beauty, love and kindness,
and leaving a legacy of true pure-heartedness in the world;
And, last of all, to my incredibly powerful, unbelievable angels,
for helping me get this book off the ground,
and teaching me how to fly!

Thank you!

I am deeply grateful for the kindness of my clients and friends who were willing to share your emotional healing stories in this book. I know that your heart-felt gift will be an incredible blessing to many others who are struggling to overcome their dysfunctional family issues. To honor your gift, your names have been changed to protect your confidentiality except in those cases where you specifically requested otherwise.

I am also very grateful for the love and support of my editor, Samuel Mahaffy, MA. Through Samuel's angelic help and guidance, *Choosing Light-Heartedness* has become much more than it ever would have been otherwise!

I am very grateful to my spiritual mentor and guide, Ione Jenson, for her continued unconditional love and encouragement in writing and publishing this book. Thank you so much!

I also want to thank Robert Bowie Johnson Jr., the author of *The Parthenon Code*, for originally encouraging me to publish *Choosing Light-Heartedness*. Even though he has never met me in person, he was willing to offer his knowledge and expertise with all my many questions about writing and publishing!

Many thanks to Jonathan Gullery for his kindness and patience and especially for the beautiful cover design! I am very grateful to have the opportunity to work with such a creative, talented and knowledgeable artist!

I am also very grateful for all those who have written about the emotional healing journey before me and paved the way for the work I am able to do today. I am especially grateful to John Bradshaw, Louise Hay, M. Scott Peck, MD, Charles Whitfield, MD, Melodie Beatie, Daniel Goleman Ph.D., Candace Pert, Ph.D., Marianne Williamson, Caroline Myss, Brian Weiss, MD, Doreen Virtue, Ph.D., Marshall Rosenburg, Ph.D., Patricia Evans, Susan Anderson, Ph.D., Ellen Bass and Laura Davis. Thank you deeply for your wisdom and for your heart!

Table of Contents

A foreword for health care professionals

There is an epidemic in society today of people who are taking anti-depressants and anti-anxiety medication to survive their emotional and psychological pain. Doctors, psychologists, and psychotherapists are regularly recommending long-term medication to deal with depression, anxiety, and dysfunctional family issues, *usually with the best of intentions*, simply because they are not familiar with the emotional healing process.

Of course, psychology, itself, is still a relatively new science since the father of psychology, Sigmund Freud, only lived and worked in the late 1800s and early 1900s. As we begin the twenty-first century, psychology as a whole has reached the point of being able to diagnose a client's problem, and recommend appropriate medications, but it hasn't yet agreed on any definitive process for helping clients actually overcome their issues. Therefore many skilled psychotherapists are still recommending psychotropic medication and teaching people coping skills for how to live with what is currently assumed to be their life-long psychological issues, rather than giving their clients the tools they need to overcome those issues.

The problem I see in the field of psychology is that we have not yet integrated spirituality with science. Quantum physics is now showing statistically that there are spiritual laws underlying scientific formulas. In the movie "What the Bleep Do We Know?" scientists from Harvard and Stanford agreed that we as human beings have access to an incredible spiritual power that can support our daily lives, if we simply choose to utilize it.

It is not necessary for professionals to convert their clients to a specific religious belief system in order to have the client use spirituality in his or her emotional healing process. Counselors or psychotherapists can simply invite their clients to find a spirituality that works for the client, and then ask him or her to incorporate it into their every day life. Alcoholics Anonymous (AA) is a wonderful example of the value of integrating spirituality with psychology, because through utilizing a spiritual approach, AA has successfully helped millions of alcoholics overcome their life-long addictions.

When psychology is integrated with spirituality, it creates a powerful healing opportunity. Psychology gives us current information about healthy self-esteem, healthy relationships, and healthy families, while spirituality gives us access to divine, unconditional love and to the Higher Power that makes spiritual healing possible. When you integrate psychology and spirituality, it becomes not only possible, but very probable that everyday people can actually overcome their emotional and psychological issues to live healthy, happy lives.

Since information about the emotional healing process has not yet been researched and documented, many clients are not told about the possibility of overcoming their emotional issues and living healthy, functioning lives. I find it very unfortunate that with all the knowledge and skills we have accumulated, many clients in every-day counseling situations are still not given clear direction for how to get from their painful, survival existence to a happy, functioning life.

Emotional healing is a natural process that occurs spontaneously when a person feels safe and supported in an open, healing environment. The doors that have been locked in a person's unconscious mind will open naturally and easily when he or she experiences the authentic compassion of an experienced professional. If a professional follows the natural healing process of a client's unconscious mind, that healing process will guide the client back to peace and happiness, much like the natural process of grief.

When a professional is trained and experienced in working with emotions, he or she can become the guiding light that guides a client through the dark, murky waters of his or her unresolved emotions. A strong, caring professional can role model emotional health and while providing the enduring kindness and compassion that is needed so a client can face the issues they have been avoiding. Unresolved feelings from the past often become much bigger and more frightening in a client's mind than what they realistically represent. Therefore the client depends on the knowledge and skill of the professional to provide safety and guidance while they feel vulnerable and out of control.

Clients who are in emotional pain need to hear from compassionate, experienced professionals that with patience and persistence it is absolutely possible to heal emotionally. They also need to be given clear guidance and direction about what they can expect to experience on their emotional healing journey. Emotional healing is not always an easy road, but when a person overcomes the pain and creates a happy, fulfilling life, it is extremely rewarding!

There are obviously many pitfalls on the journey to emotional health and many times where it would be easier for a client to give up and take medication to numb the pain than to continue working through the emotional issues that arise. I am not suggesting, of course, that professionals should never recommend psychotropic medication. Clearly there are times when it is necessary.

I like to think of psychotropic medication as a short-term help for clients who are suicidal or in severe crisis when used along with counseling or psychotherapy, while the client is learning the important skills needed for living without it. The problem with prescribing medication on a long-term basis is that anti-depressants have only been available for the past twenty years and anti-anxiety medications only a few years more. We have not yet had time to research the long-term effect of these medications on our physical health.

In her groundbreaking book, *Molecules of Emotion,* Dr. Candace Pert tells of her scientific research on how chemicals inside our bodies form an information network linking our minds and our bodies and therefore also affecting our physical health. Dr. Pert concludes from her research that emotional and spiritual tools are a better alternative for dealing with psychological issues than psychotropic medication, because of the impact psychological denial and unresolved emotions have on our physical health.

I believe that although anti-depressants and anti-anxiety medications are often a necessary tool to meet short-term psychological needs, taking high doses of medication to numb emotional pain on a long-term basis will never bring a person to that experience of inner peace, joy and fulfillment that they are seeking. Only a holistic approach that includes body, mind and spirit will accomplish that goal.

I have written *Choosing Lightheartedness* as a psychological and spiritual guide for everyday people who want to take that journey from emotional pain and suffering to emotional health and happiness. It is my hope that both professionals and clients will refer to it as a guide for releasing emotional pain and suffering to create happy, functioning lives!

Before we begin....

Hello! Welcome to this exciting 33-day journey. I'm so happy that you're here! We're going to have a wonderful time together. Maybe that's hard for you to believe right now and that's okay. You may think that it's difficult for someone to be genuine and real or sincerely compassionate through a book. I do understand! All I ask is that you set your doubts aside for a short time and embark on the emotional healing journey that I'm offering. When it's complete, you can tell me if you believe my sincerity. Is that okay with you?

The most important thing I want you to know up front is that you are a very special person. I happen to know that there is something uniquely wonderful about you. You are special and beautiful in ways that you haven't even discovered! You may be wondering if I'm totally crazy right now, but trust me, I know that before this month is over you'll be saying "She was right! How did she know that?" Are you smiling? I am, because I know it's true!

I also want you to know is that no matter what has happened to you in your life, it's never too late to change directions and turn you life around. Your life could be very rich, rewarding and fulfilling if you simply choose to do the work it takes to heal emotionally. I won't pretend that *Choosing Lightheartedness* is a simple, one step process. It's a complex healing journey that will undoubtedly challenge you at times, but I don't know anyone who's tried it that really wants to go back to how their life used to be.

I'm writing this book for you because many years ago I was also anxious and depressed. The truth is I was miserable and lonely, and I didn't know what to do to get better. The information I'm going to share with you in this book was not available back then. I had to learn everything from scratch and fall on my face many times and pick myself up again and again

1

before I even got a taste of peace and happiness. So I'm writing this book for you now so that you won't have to go through what I did. I know how painful that can be and I wouldn't wish it on anyone.

Something else I think you should know is that I know, without a doubt, that you have something very important to do in the world. *Whether you are a millionaire sitting in a mountain top villa when you read this book or a prisoner in a jail cell, I absolutely know that you have an important purpose to fulfill!* Maybe you can already feel the truth of what I'm saying or maybe you are feeling a little skeptical. I wouldn't blame you a bit for being skeptical. I have always been a "seeing is believing" kind of person myself.

I'll bet some of you are hoping that I know what I'm talking about. Good for you! That means you have an open mind and you are willing to be shown the truth if it, in fact, proves to be truth. Great! One thing you can count on with me is that I'm an honest person. I won't tell you anything unless I know it's true. I would never in a million years want to add to your pain! I know that if you're reading this book that you've already suffered enough.

Maybe you're saying, "Listen you've got the wrong person! I bought your book because I'm feeling depressed or anxious. I'm reading it to try to get better myself, not to save the whole world along with me!" It's okay, I do understand. I know it will take time for you to see the truth of what I'm saying. I'm not asking you to believe me right now. I'm just asking that you try to keep an open mind.

I just want you to know that you and I have a lot more to do together than just getting you past your anxiety or depression. You've got a whole new life ahead of you! You and I need to roll up our sleeves and get to work because we've got to get you ready for it!

Anxiety and Depression

So before we begin, I want to clarify for you my personal beliefs about the symptoms of anxiety and depression, which are based on my therapy work over the past twenty-five years with people who have had these symptoms. I do believe that we are genetically inclined toward particular symptoms. For example, if you suffer from anxiety or depression, there are probably other people in your ancestral family who also had anxiety or depression. We're now learning that a tendency towards anxiety or depression is probably carried genetically, in the same way that a tendency toward cancer or heart disease is carried genetically.

But, in the same way that we are also now discovering that with proper diet and exercise we can affect our genetic predisposition towards cancer and heart disease, I believe that with proper *emotional diet and exercise*, we can also affect our tendency to be anxious and depressed. In other words, I do not believe that just because one or both of your parents suffered from anxiety or depression, that you are destined to fight anxiety or depression for the rest of your life.

I know from my own experience, and from the experiences of thousands of clients over the years, that even with the genetic predisposition towards anxiety and depression, you can greatly decrease the severity of the symptom you have taken on, or even release it completely. To do so, you must be determined and persistent in your commitment to emotional healing.

It is my belief that if you suffer from anxiety or depression, you have taken on a symptom that began many years ago when you were just a small child. Even if you are genetically inclined towards this symptom, I believe that the environment you were raised in as a child greatly affected how severe the anxiety or depression became for you. I have learned from my experience in working with anxiety and depression that if you go back and resolve the emotional issues that began in your dysfunctional childhood, your anxiety and depression will greatly decrease or go away completely.

If you would like some validation of what I'm saying, read the stories in this book or go to my website at www.kari-joys.com and read some of the testimonials. There are three different sets of testimonials on the website. You'll find them under *Sessions with Kari, Personal Growth Workshops and Yuen Method Wellness*. These are stories of ordinary people who have experienced the miracle of emotional healing through this work.

Releasing your symptoms

I chose not to focus on your symptoms in this book, but rather to focus on the *cause* of the symptoms, which is where the symptoms began and where they can also be released. The only purpose I see for checking in on your symptoms from time to time is to validate the progress you are making towards healing. *You will know if you are getting to the real issues in your emotional healing journey when your symptoms start to decrease!*

Verbal, physical and sexual abuse

I would also like to point out that although I refer to dysfunctional families and childhood abuse many times in this book, I have not focused specifically on one type of childhood abuse such as verbal, physical, or sexual abuse. I could easily write an entire book on recovering from any of these types of abuse, but for the purpose of your healing right now, I chose the parts of the emotional healing process that are general to all dysfunctional family issues.

I want you to know that this is not because I think that your specific type of abuse is unimportant. If you were abused verbally, physically, or sexually as a child, the scars of that abuse will be with you forever, even after you heal the emotional pain. They are never to be taken lightly.

If you follow the process of *Choosing Lightheartedness*, the homework you do will make your experience specific to your particular type of childhood abuse. Working through the feelings of anger, sadness and hurt from your particular abuse is crucial to your emotional healing. I would strongly encourage you to also read other books on verbal, physical, and sexual abuse, and I will suggest some of them to you throughout this book.

How this book works

So let's talk a bit about how this book works and what you can expect from it. There are actually 17 chapters in this process, but I've scheduled them over 33 days because, as you will soon find out, *Choosing Lightheartedness* is packed with learning tools and information that would normally take an intelligent person at least six months to digest emotionally. If you try to do it too quickly, you could easily be overwhelmed and give up before you complete it.

I realize that no one follows a book exactly the way it's written, but I'm requesting that for your own best interest you take this process slowly and really digest each section before you go on to the next one. I would suggest that you read each entire chapter completely and thoroughly on each of the two days given, because often the information itself is often more than you can take in emotionally on the first day you read it. *What we're attempting to do here is heal your emotional body, not just your mind. Emotional healing is much more complex than intellectual healing.*

Then I'd suggest that you do the homework during the two days given for that chapter so that you can complete it before you go on to the next chapter. If you want to get the results that I'm suggesting, don't skip over parts of the homework. It's better to just take extra days if you need them. Please remember that this is not an informational book. It's a journey that will change your life if you allow it to.

Every lesson gives you just enough information so that you can do the homework and actually experience what I'm describing by delving into your own heart, your own feelings, and your own life. *If you try to do it as information only, it will become dull and boring. Your life is what makes it fascinating, because, believe it or not, you are fascinating!*

When you follow the process I'm describing and actually practice it in your own life, you will see changes that will amaze and astonish you. There will definitely be times when you feel overwhelmed and you want to give up and quit, but please resist that impulse! It's very important that you make a commitment to yourself before you begin to do whatever it takes to complete this process.

Finding support for this process

It is extremely important for most people to have emotional support in this emotional healing process. There are several ways you can find that support if you need it. You could plan to take this 33-day journey with a good friend. If you choose that, it's important to make a commitment to get together or talk on the phone daily to support each other along the way. True friendship can help tremendously in your emotional healing journey. I would never have survived my own emotional healing without my dearest, life-long friend.

If you do chose to do this process with a friend, you will need to make a commitment up front not to judge each other along the way or give each other advice. You may not always agree with how your friend does things and that's okay. Just make a commitment to practice giving pure, unconditional love to your friend in the best way you know.

Often the greatest gift you can give your friend is just to listen and care. You don't have to have the answers for his or her problems. Just let them know that you believe in their ability to overcome their challenges and that you'll be there, cheering him or her on all the way through this emotional healing journey! Remember that a true friend is one of the most valuable gifts you'll ever receive in the world.

Another option for finding support would be to take this book with you and find a caring mental health professional in your area who would be willing to support your healing process. Be sure to ask your psychotherapist *before you start* if they are familiar with emotional healing or if they would be willing to read the book along with you and support your experience.

If those options don't work for you, you could plan to attend one of my *Personal Growth Workshops*. Check my website at www.kari-joys.com and you'll find the information you need to contact me.

Suicidal feelings

The emotional healing process involved in *Choosing Lightheartedness* is not appropriate to use without professional guidance and support if you are suicidal or if you are severely depressed. You can make use of this material, but you will need a caring mental health professional to support you in the process.

If at any time during the 33-day process you encounter suicidal feelings, it is of ultimate importance that you get professional help immediately! Call 911 in your area, call the mental health hotline,

or go to the nearest hospital and ask to be evaluated. It's never worth it to risk your life because you are afraid of what's inside you. Your life is very precious! You have so much to do on this planet that you absolutely can't do without a body. Take yourself seriously and get help immediately!

Important beliefs and practices you need to adopt

If you intend to take the emotional healing journey and be successful, I believe that there are a number of beliefs and practices you must adopt in order to succeed. I've included a few of them here for your benefit. *You may need to refer back to these thoughts from time to time, if you ever feel like your train is derailing on your journey back to emotional health and happiness.*

1. It is absolutely possible to heal emotionally, no matter what happened to you in your life. You can definitely create a life that feels rich, rewarding and fulfilling to you.

2. Your most important task is to imagine yourself emotionally healthy and happy for five minutes every day until you get there. It's important to imagine it in living color, using all of your five senses, and let yourself really feel what it would be like for you to be healthy and happy. When you encounter resistance or obstacles along the way, always come back to imagining yourself healthy and happy, and then simply watch what happens in your life!

3. When you are imagining yourself healthy and happy on a daily basis, your inner guidance will guide you, step by step, through your own intuition to do what you need to do each day to achieve your goal. If you pay attention, your intuition will tell you which books to read, which teachers to learn from, and which counselors or psychotherapists to work with so that you can achieve emotional health and happiness more quickly.

4. If you want to heal emotionally, you will have to own your power and take charge of your own healing process. Don't give your power to your doctor, your psychotherapist, your minister, or anyone else, and expect them to heal you, and don't blame them if you don't get what you think you need. *No one is responsible for your emotional healing but you!* If you're not happy with the help you're getting, just move on, follow your intuition and find what you need elsewhere.

5. Learning to take care of your body is part of your emotional healing journey. It would be very helpful for you to get out in nature and walk 30-45 minutes a day while you take this 33-day journey. Research shows that the affect of exercising three times a week is comparable to taking an antidepressant.

6. You may have to give up all your favorite opinions and beliefs about yourself, about other people, and about life itself in the process of emotional healing. Old opinions and beliefs are often part of your adapted, false self rather than the true self that you were really meant to be. Opinions often get in the way of your growth, while feelings will help you move on through the challenge.

7. The quality of willingness is crucial for you to develop. You have to be willing to grow and change every day, even at times when growing becomes very uncomfortable for you. If willingness is difficult for you, you can always ask for divine help and pray for willingness to be willing.

8. The quality of surrender is also crucial. You have to remember that you are not in charge of the healing process, and you don't get to decide when you've grown enough! Let your Higher Power guide your emotional healing journey and show you what you need to do to continue healing. When you are truly happy and healthy, it will be obvious to you and to everyone around you. Until then, keep growing!

9. Personal growth is never as bad as you think it's going to be. It's the anticipation of the pain that hurts the most. If you face your fear and move through it, the monster you've created will always take off it's mask.

10. Forgiveness is a very important part of emotional healing. Of course, the hardest person to forgive is often your self, but forgiveness of self and others is a requirement for emotional health.

11. Learning to give unconditional love to your self and others is also very important. The hardest person to love may also be your self, but self-love is definitely a requirement for emotional health.

12. Vulnerability is a sign of great strength, not a sign of weakness. When you can learn to feel safe in your vulnerability, it actually demonstrates great progress in your emotional healing journey. Emotional healing may well be the most important journey you ever take, and you definitely cannot heal emotionally without allowing yourself to be vulnerable.

13. Although this book is based on a 33-day journey, your lifetime emotional healing journey will not be complete in thirty-three days. What *Choosing Lightheartedness* provides is to give you the important steps in the emotional healing journey. If you follow the homework that is provided, this 33-day journey will bring you to a feeling of joy, hope and lightheartedness.

14. When you have completed the original thirty-three days, you will need to continue your personal healing journey by referring back to the different chapters in this book on an 'as needed' basis. You will know when you have gone off track from your healthy, true self when you start to feel anxious or depressed like you did in the past.

You can bring yourself back on track by reviewing the various chapters provided in this book. Your intuition will tell you which ones to refer back to at any given time. You can also go more in depth on any of these chapters by reading the other books that are referred to in the homework following each chapter. If none of that is working for you, you may need professional help and guidance. Don't ever be afraid to pursue professional help when you need it!

15. The good news is that all of your needs will be provided along the way as long as you are willing to keep learning and growing. *I know from many years of experience that God smiles on people who demonstrate a willingness to grow!* Ask God and your angels for help when you need it, and then keep your heart and your mind open to your inner guidance. If you are asking for spiritual help and guidance, you will always receive the love and support you need even though it often doesn't come the way you expect it.

Never give up!

I truly believe that this process will be an incredible joy to you if you hang in there and take it slowly. Watching our lives change before our eyes is a monumental experience. You will feel at times like you're on a roller coaster of emotions, but if you hang in there, you'll be amazed and delighted at the end result!

Just remember never to give up on your emotional healing. With time, patience and persistence, you absolutely can create a life that is better than anything you can even imagine right now. When you reach inner peace and happiness, it will be worth everything you've put into the process of growth, and so much more! You'll be absolutely thrilled with the joy, peace and lightheartedness that you experience for the rest of your life!

I wish you much love, light and laughter on your journey!

Love and de-light, Kari

Chapter One

Why Do I Always Feel Different and Not Good Enough?

Jennifer

When Jennifer first came to therapy she was very lost and depressed. She hardly spoke for the first few months. Little by little we pieced together her story. She was abandoned at birth and given up for adoption. She spent several months in a children's home and then a nice family with four other children adopted her.

Jennifer had a relatively pleasant childhood, but she had no sense of her self. She never felt "good enough" in any situation. Her adoptive mother had never validated her feelings and had made every decision for her. When Jennifer grew up and wanted to go to college and become a physician, her mother said it wasn't necessary and she should get married and have babies instead. When Jennifer's new husband had an affair the first month of her marriage, her mother said she had to stay in the marriage, because, after all, what would people think?

Soon after she came to therapy, Jennifer began asking me what decisions she should make. I told her she would have to decide for herself, because it was her life, not mine. At first she was shocked and terrified, but as she began working through her "not-good-enough" feelings and learning how to love her self unconditionally, the decisions she made began to pay off.

Jennifer went back to school and finished her undergraduate degree and graduated with honors. She bought a house and worked out room by room how to remodel it. She raised two healthy, happy sons and became the Mom that all the neighborhood teenagers loved to spend time with.

Today Jennifer is happy and healthy. She's fun and light-hearted, in fact, you'd never know she was ever depressed. Jennifer will tell you today that her life is much better than she ever thought was possible before. She'll tell you that her healing journey was a challenge, but she's very pleased with the results!

Days 1 and 2

First I want to welcome you to this incredible journey! If you follow the plan I am offering you, your life will never be the same. Healing anxiety, depression, poor self esteem, childhood abuse and other dysfunctional family issues can often take a lifetime, but after working with survivors of dysfunctional families for the past twenty-five years, I know that I can make it much quicker and easier for you. I've broken down the steps of emotional healing into bite-sized chunks, so that anyone, *including you*, can understand it and do what it takes. So hang on to your seats! This roller coaster ride is taking off. Don't worry; it's going to be an exciting adventure!

If you grew up in a dysfunctional family, you may have sometimes wondered why you are different from everyone else and why your life doesn't work the way it's supposed to. You may have felt like you're just "not good enough" in some way, like maybe you were born with the sign "Damaged Goods" on your forehead.

Maybe you have had relationships that failed, or maybe you tried to accomplish things that were always just out of reach. Maybe your friends have rejected you again and again, or maybe you continually find yourself at the point of wanting to give up and crawl into a little hole some-where. Relax! You're not alone. People who grew up in dysfunctional fam-ilies often feel that way.

There is a very good reason why your life hasn't worked the way you wanted it to. Remember that psychology is a new science. Freud, the father of psychology, only lived in the late 1800s and early 1900s. It's only much more recently, since the 1980s and 1990s that psychology has evolved to the point of actually having the information we need to resolve our emotional issues. As a culture, we didn't acknowledge the value and importance of early childhood nurturing until the 1990s. We didn't real-ize that how we were treated as a child greatly determines our emotional and psychological health.

So even if you had two parents who loved you the best way they knew and even if your physical needs were met as a child; the informa-tion for how to raise happy, healthy children with good self esteem sim-ply wasn't available at that time, even to the most well-meaning parents. And then when it became available, there was a huge controversy in our culture about whether it was really important or necessary, or whether the old ways of raising children were better than the new. Many parents got caught in the struggle of doing what society expected or approved of, even when their hearts told them differently.

It is only since the 1980s and 1990s that we as a culture are evolv-ing to the point of understanding the psychological importance of how we raise our children. Unfortunately, we have now just barely begun to put into action the information we have to change the way we live. So it's highly unlikely that you were taught as a child that you were valuable as a person, that your feelings and needs were important, and that there was a way to communicate and resolve conflict in your family that could be loving and respectful to everyone involved.

Children think that the world revolves around them. If everything is happy and positive in their world, they think that they are special, won-derful little human beings. But if there is ugliness, or abuse, or disharmony in their lives, they also think that the ugliness is because of them, and that it means they are bad, or not good enough in some way. So if your fam-ily was anything like the norm, where there was alcoholism, verbal, physical, or sexual abuse, or simply stressful circumstances that were out of everyone's control, you probably grew up feeling like you were bad and that there was something wrong with you.

Even if your parents felt incredible love for you as a child, they simply didn't have the information they needed to love you the way you needed to be loved, which includes helping you understand your own value and worth as a human being, and helping you express your feelings and your needs in healthy ways. If one or both of your parents were physically, verbally, or sexually abusive, expressing your feelings and needs as a child was probably completely impossible.

It's sad, but normal for children who don't feel loved the way they need to be loved and who aren't encouraged to express their emotional needs to internalize those unexpressed feelings and unmet needs. Often they will become anxious or depressed, or sometimes act out their unresolved feelings and unmet needs later in life in ways that are destructive to themselves or others.

So what you and I are going to do together is undo the emotional damage that was done to you, even if it was done in the name of love by the most well-intentioned parents. *I want to help you really get it at a gut level that you are a beautiful, incredible human being, and that no matter how badly you have been hurt, or how severely you have hurt other people, it's never too late to change.* You always have the opportunity, at any moment, to completely change the direction of your life.

I'm not going to tell you that all of this journey will be easy and effortless. What I said earlier was that I can help you make it much easier than if you tried to do it on your own. Looking at yourself honestly and doing the work it takes to change your life is never just a piece of cake. It's difficult, and challenging, and scary at times. But the good news is that it's never more than you can handle. There are always ways to get what you need along the way, but you have to take the first step. No one can do it but you!

So let's get started. What you need first of all is a journal. I personally like writing in an old-fashioned spiral notebook because you can take it with you if you go for a walk or a drive, or if you want to sit by a lake or a stream, but if you prefer writing on your computer, that's okay too.

The first step to emotional health and learning to live lightheartedly is learning to be your own best friend. Writing in your journal will teach you over time how to do be your own best friend. Writing about your inner experience gets you through a lot of challenging feelings. Your journal will be a living record of your own journey from anxiety and depression to fun and lightheartedness. It's a record that you can keep for the rest of your life. As time goes on, it will help you see your own progress, and before long you'll actually start to feel like a lighthearted person.

For today, I suggest you go out in nature somewhere to do your homework. It's so much easier to feel the energy of the Universe and your Higher Power when you're out in nature. I'd like you to find a place where you can breathe the fresh air, and hear the birds, and see the beauty of the natural world all around you. If for any reason you can't go outdoors, close your eyes and imagine yourself walking out in nature, or sitting by a stream, or lying on your back and watching the clouds like you did when you were a child before you start this exercise.

There are several parts to your assignment today. The first part is to write a paragraph about your present symptoms. What are the things you want to change through this process? Are you anxious or depressed? Do you have poor self-esteem? Does your childhood abuse still affect you today? Write a paragraph or two about how those symptoms are affecting your life today.

Next I'd like you to make a list of all the ways your life isn't working or hasn't worked in the past. Write down your challenges, your disappointments, your so-called failures, the people who rejected you, the people you don't speak to any more, and the reasons they are out of your life; write down what is wrong with your life and why you are so convinced that you aren't "good enough."

Be very specific about what you're writing, and please be honest. We won't get anywhere together if you can't learn to be honest with yourself. By the way, there's no one to fool on this journey you're taking, except yourself! If you want to be your own best friend, wouldn't you rather have a friend who's honest?

When you are finished with those questions, we'll go on to the next one. This time I want you to write a few paragraphs on how you would like your life to be. If someone could wave a magic wand and paint your life a different color, what color would you paint it? Or, in other words, if your life could take a dramatic change for the better, how would you want it to change?

Again, be very honest and be specific! What do you think it would take to help you feel more happy and light-hearted? Would you want material things, like a new house and a new car, and maybe a better job that would pay for all of that? Would you want a healthier, happier marriage? Would you want better self-esteem or more self worth? Would you want a happy, healthy family, or deep, meaningful friendships?

So let's get started and write it all down, and when you've finished, please read over what you've written. Some day you're going to be looking back on this writing as the living record of the beginning of your new life!

Homework Assignment: Chapter One

1. Find a journal that you can use for this journey. You can either buy a spiral notebook that you can take with you anywhere or use your computer if you prefer. Remember, your journal is an important part of this journey because it will help you learn to be your own best friend!

2. If possible, go out in nature to do this journaling process. Go for a walk or a drive and find a peaceful, comfortable place to sit and write, where you can breathe the fresh air, hear the birds singing, and see the beauty of nature around you. If you can't go outside for any reason, before you start this exercise close your eyes and imagine walking out in nature, or sitting by a stream, or lying on your back and watching the clouds like you did when you were a child.

3. Write a paragraph about your present symptoms and how they are affecting you as an adult. Write about your anxiety, your depression, your poor self-esteem, or how your childhood verbal, physical,

or sexual abuse is still affecting you today.

4.   Write a list of what is wrong with your life. Include your failed rela-
     tionships, your challenges, your disappointments, your so-called fail-
     ures in life, the people who rejected you, the people you don't speak
     to any more, and the reasons they are out of your life; write down
     very clearly what is wrong with your life, and why you are so con-
     vinced that you aren't "good enough." Be honest, be specific, and
     be complete!

5.   Write a few paragraphs on how you would like your life to be. If
     your life could take a dramatic change for the better, how would
     you want it to change? What do you think would help you feel more
     happy and lighthearted? Would you want material things, like a new
     house and a new car, and maybe a job that pays for all of that? Would
     you want a healthier, happier marriage? Would you want better self-
     esteem or self worth? Would you want a happy, healthy family, or
     deep, meaningful friendships? Take your time. Be sure you've really
     outlined the life you want clearly and in detail!

6.   Now write a few pages in your journal about how you feel today
     after doing today's homework. Use the hot-pen technique, where
     you just write, write, write. In other words, just let your stream of
     consciousness flow. Don't censor anything! Focus on what you're
     feeling as much as you can, because getting in touch with your feel-
     ings is what will help you heal emotionally. This journal is just for
     you, and the best way to get to know yourself deeply is just to let
     yourself write anything and everything that comes to your mind.

*Hey, good job! We're off to a good start! You're going to love this heal-
ing journey! Just remember to stay on schedule and take each lesson one at
a time. If you try to do it all at once, you could easily get overwhelmed.*

Chapter Two

Uncover the Truth about How Your Childhood Affected Your Self-Esteem!

David

David was born the youngest of four children in a typical blended American family. Everything changed when David was two years old because his parents divorced and his father kidnapped David and his brother and left town. David's father changed his son's names so that his mother couldn't ever find them, so David never really met his Mom until he was seventeen. He grew up knowing that his Dad was alcoholic and verbally and physically abusive, but when you grow up that way, you tend to think it's normal.

David graduated from college in his twenties and got a job in his chosen profession. He had a long-term relationship with a nice young woman whom he thought he loved. Everything looked right on the outside so he couldn't understand why he felt so miserable and depressed on the inside. He was at a friend's house one night when the subject of dysfunctional families came up and suddenly David was overpowered with intense feelings he couldn't understand. He had never before realized the emotional impact of his childhood.

After the emotional dam broke, David's memories and feelings came pouring out uncontrollably. Sometimes he felt completely crazy because the flashbacks were so intense and so extreme! As the pieces of the puzzle came together, David realized that he had been verbally, physically and sexually abused, not only by his own father, but also by strangers who paid his matronly babysitter for sexual favors from little David.

David's emotional healing journey was challenging and overwhelming at times. At times he felt hopeless and suicidal, and at other times he was blissfully happy and tremendously relieved. It felt so freeing for David to finally know what was wrong. For several years he came to my therapy groups and personal growth workshops regularly. He had such deep, excruciating pain to release!

Finally the pain began to subside and David began to see himself and his life through new eyes. The colors of flowers suddenly looked brighter and more beautiful. Music was richer and more harmonious. Life became exciting and inviting, with amazing new experiences to look forward to every day.

David says his life today is radically different than it was before. He's now happily married to a lovely woman. He has many wonderful friends and a large support system. He says he has never felt so much love in his entire life! He laughs regularly and finds joy spontaneously in every situation.

Although he doesn't work in the field of counseling, David says his highest priority at this point in his life is to return the gift that was offered to him when he was in emotional pain. He feels very lucky to have had the opportunity to heal the past and he wants to give other people who are hurting the incredible opportunity for emotional healing that was given to him!

Days 3 and 4

Hello! Welcome back! You probably thought we would get to the fun part by today, right? It's true, we will! When you start to experience the ah-ha's and the breakthroughs that come from emotional healing, it all starts to be fun, because you feel so much more free and light-hearted! It's like taking a load of bricks off your back that you've been carrying for a lifetime, and realizing you don't have to carry them anymore. It makes you want to jump up and down for joy, and run and play and do cartwheels like a child!

There are two secrets about this process that I'm going to share with you today. The first secret is that you can't go over the mountain or around the mountain; you have to go through the mountain. *In other words, you can't go over your issues or around your issues. If you want to be emotionally healthy and authentically light-hearted, you will have to deal with your issues directly.*

The only way to heal your anxiety, your depression or your dysfunctional family issues is to face the issues head on. All that denial and avoidance that you've tried in the past obviously didn't work, or you wouldn't be here right now. So before we move on, you may as well face the truth that if you want to feel truly light-hearted, you'll have to do the work it takes to get there!

But here's the good news! Are you ready? *The second secret is that the pain that you've been avoiding all these years is never as bad as you think it's going to be.* Too often you drink, and do drugs, and become workaholics, and get addicted to all kinds of other things because you're so terrified of facing your own pain, only to find out in the end that it was a big waste of time and energy, because the pain wasn't nearly as bad as you thought it would be. You could have been through the worst of it in a year easily, if you had simply made the commitment to doing the work to heal the pain. After making that commitment, all you have to do is get started and then keep on trucking on down the road until you get there!

So let's move forward. If you suffer from anxiety, depression, poor self-esteem, or the affects of childhood abuse you probably know you grew up in a dysfunctional family. But do you understand exactly what that means? There are different levels of dysfunctional families, from the mildly dysfunctional families we talked about yesterday that simply didn't have the information they needed to raise healthy children to the more severely dysfunctional families, which we will discuss more in depth today.

If you grew up in a severely dysfunctional family, one or both parents of your parents were probably addicted to alcohol, drugs, food, sex, relationships, gambling, religion, workaholism or control. You may have been verbally, physically or sexually abused at a young age. More than likely your parents were so overwhelmed with life or so self-centered that they were not interested or able to meet your physical and emotional needs.

If you came from a severely dysfunctional family, you were probably not encouraged to be yourself or to express your feelings and needs. More than likely your family lacked the qualities of honesty, integrity, love, harmony and respect. You probably were not able to develop healthy self-esteem or a strong sense of who you were as a person. You may have learned to survive the emotional pain and suffering in your family by developing symptoms like anxiety or depression or by developing survival skills like denial, dishonesty, manipulation or control. Often you didn't realize what was wrong or why you felt the way you did.

Children who grew up in severely dysfunctional families tend to have many deep emotional issues that keep them stuck in emotional ruts later in life. Many times you don't know who you are, don't know what you want to do with your life, or don't know how to get there. You tend to sabotage yourself and find yourself going through the same patterns over and over and over and yet you never understand what you're doing wrong. Often you tell yourself that it's the other people in your life who are hurting you still today, even though you may have noticed that you are the only common denominator in the on-going dramas that you are creating.

There are many books on dysfunctional families that you can read that will help you get a more in-depth understanding of the issue, if you haven't read them already. If you need to brush up on that information, you can go to your public library or to your local bookstore and browse through some books on dysfunctional families. One of the original books written on the topic was the book *Codependent No More* by Melodie Beatie. Her book describes the characteristics of codependence and it is still very popular today.

The term 'codependent' originally came from the Alcoholics Anonymous movement, and it referred to children who grew up in alcoholic families, who had to live their life around an alcoholic and always gauge their activities on whether the alcoholic was drunk, or whether he/she was having a good day or a bad day. As the AA movement progressed, it was found that some other families seemed to have some of the same issues even if no one in the family was alcoholic, and so the name 'dysfunctional family' was coined. As time went on and more research was done, we discovered that most families are dysfunctional to some degree, and the question no longer is whether your family was dysfunctional, but how dysfunctional was it?

So if you grew up in a severely dysfunctional family you probably share many common characteristics of other codependent adults, like low self-esteem or low self worth, poor boundaries, poor communication skills, feeling like a victim, intense neediness or dependency, lack of trust, denial, manipulation and control. Many of you probably became anxious and depressed, isolated and withdrawn, and perhaps even suicidal.

It all goes back to what we discussed earlier. In the early 1900s, people believed that if you gave your children food to eat, and clothes to wear, and put a roof over their head, you were doing a good job as a parent. People didn't have time to even think about issues like self-esteem or higher quality of life. They were far too busy trying to physically survive the best way they could. It wasn't until after the 1950s that we had time and energy to started questioning the way things had always been done, and why we weren't happy, or why we were not able to enjoy all the luxury we had created.

It was only in the 1980's and 1990s that everyday people started talking about things like dysfunctional families, or domestic violence, or physical, verbal, or sexual abuse. You simply didn't talk about those things before. You just accepted the fate you had been given, whatever it was, and tried to make the best of your life. Before that time no one realized that children need unconditional love and emotional support. No one understood the importance of helping children express their feelings and their needs. No one had the necessary information to understand what creates healthy self-esteem.

Don't get me wrong, I'm not excusing the people who hurt you as a child. I believe that there was always an innate understanding about right and wrong and about treating people with love and kindness. Christ, as well as many other great spiritual teachers, taught the spiritual principals of love and kindness thousands of year ago. For people who were committed to living their spirituality, the spiritual principals were always available.

What was not available back then was the knowledge of how to live those spiritual principals on a daily basis. Parents, who had been emotionally traumatized or damaged themselves, didn't know what to do to get past their own issues. In fact, no one had the understanding it took to undo his or her own emotional damage once it was done. Many times, these emotionally wounded people went through their lives being miserable, acting out their own emotional pain, and traumatizing and wounding many more innocent children in the process.

If you were one of those sweet, innocent children who was severely abused or neglected, I just want you to know that I am truly sorry. It is very sad to me that we live in a culture that can build huge skyscrapers and send people to the moon, but we don't know how to love our own children and give them the basic nurturing, and guidance, and support they need to become healthy, happy, functioning adults!

I also want you to know that what you deserved as a child was so much more than abuse and neglect. *Whether or not your parents were willing or able to love you unconditionally or treat you with the honor and respect you deserved when you came into the world, you absolutely deserved it!* Loving a child unconditionally is actually very simple when your parents are loving and healthy themselves. But to emotionally damaged parents, providing unconditional love seems to be an insurmountable task.

But remember, the good news is that no matter what happened to you, it's never too late to heal and turn your life around! I've witnessed thousands of people before you doing just that. The stories people tell me are very different, but the feelings are always the same. What we all needed as children was just that pure, unconditional love that our wounded parents simply didn't know how to provide.

If you are willing to practice the skills I teach you, I know that I can help you learn how to love yourself and love that sweet innocent little child inside you. When you do the tasks I suggest for you, you will heal emotionally! Isn't that an exciting thought?

Learning to love your inner child is not a simple task, however, especially for those of you who came from severely dysfunctional families. It does take time and effort, but you can absolutely do it if you are determined and persistent. *Luckily, your unconscious mind doesn't know the difference between you loving the child within yourself or having that love come from other sources.* So the love you give yourself today goes into your unconscious mind just like the love a healthy parent would give to their cherished, innocent child.

Today and tomorrow we're going to take a look at what really happened in your childhood that affected your self-esteem, because that's the only way emotional healing will occur. We're not going to spend years mucking around in the swamp and blaming your parents for your life, we're just going to face the honest truth and deal with it, so that you can heal the past and make your life in the present what you really want it to be.

Okay, it's time for us to get to work. Please get out your journal or go to your computer. We're going to do some delving into your past. I'd like you to try not to answer my questions too quickly. Please do some real deep thinking about your answers. Remember that it's not an accident that you are where you are in your life. There is always a reason. If you want your life to get better, and if you want to feel authentic joy and light-heartedness, you have to be willing to do the work it takes to undo the emotional damage. So let's get busy! Are you ready?

Homework Assignment: Chapter Two

1. I'd like you to answer some questions about your childhood:
    A. What is your first memory as a child? I'd like you to write a paragraph about that memory and about your feelings while you are

in that memory.

B. Please describe for me your relationship to your mother as a young child when you were under ten years old.

C. Now describe your relationship to your father as a young child, also when you were under ten years old.

D. If there were any other caregivers in your life as a young child, describe your relationship to them as well.

E. Was anyone in your family alcoholic when you were a child?

F. Describe any abuse in your childhood. Was it physical, sexual, or verbal abuse? How severe was it? How old were you when it happened? Did anyone help you deal with the abuse? Did anyone tell you it wasn't your fault?

2. Please think for a moment about how your family dealt with feelings and needs, and then answer these questions:

A. Were you encouraged to express your feelings? Did your parents teach you how to do that?

B. Did your parents role-model healthy communication of feelings and healthy conflict resolution in your family?

C. What happened when you asked for what you needed as a child? Were your parents concerned about your needs?

D. What did you need that you didn't get as a child? Please think deeply and write about your physical, emotional, intellectual and spiritual needs.

3. Either today or tomorrow, I'd like you to write a letter in your daily journal to your Mom and Dad or to your early caregivers, and tell them what it was like for you growing up as a child in that environment. Tell them how you felt about it then, and how you feel about it now that you have a better understanding of how it has affected you.

   Don't worry about being nice or understanding right now. You can say anything you want to say in your journal. This is a place to tell the truth about the pain that is still left inside you. Tell them about how their choices affected your adult life! You're not going to mail this to them, so it won't hurt them in any way. You're writing it simply for your own benefit. Writing about your feelings helps you to feel and release the emotional pain that is still left from what happened back then.

4. When your letter is complete, I'd like you to do a little exercise with me. I want you to find a mirror, and sit down comfortably to do this process. Are you ready? Okay, I want you to look deeply into your own eyes in the mirror like you would look in the eyes of someone you love, like a dear friend, or like your own son or daughter. I want you to use your own first name and say these words to yourself "_____, *I love you, just the way you are!*"

    I'd like you to say those words to yourself over and over for a few minutes. *Say it at least ten times.* I want you to practice really meaning what you say. Say it like you'd say it to someone that you love a lot, or like you'd say it to your own son or daughter. If it feels phony to you right now, say it anyway, because in time you will start to believe it.

5. Next, I want you to do a process that I learned from an old friend of mine named Sally Pierone. Sally is a very fun, lighthearted person! She taught me to do this process years ago and it really helped. What you do is find a calendar and a red pen and hang them next to a mirror that you use regularly. Every morning and evening, you say those same words to your self again; "_____*I love you, just the way you are!*" In the morning, when you say them, draw a heart on the calendar, and in the evening fill in the heart with the red pen.

    The goal is to get 21 days in a row of little red hearts. If you miss a day, you have to start over, but keep going till you get 21 days in a row. It only takes 21 days to change a habit, so when you get the 21 days straight, your unconscious mind will be in the new habit of loving yourself! *This process is very powerful! Remember that your unconscious mind doesn't know the difference between you loving the child inside yourself, or someone else loving him or her!*

6. Okay, you're doing great! Here's the next step. Sometime today or tomorrow, I'd like you to go buy yourself a bouquet of your favorite flowers to thank you and your inner child for beginning this very important journey. When you look at the flowers throughout the day, just remember to say "thank-you" to yourself and to that sweet little person inside you. Remember that what you're doing here will affect you for the rest of your life. This may well be the most important journey you ever take!

7. There are some books you may want to read to support your healing process. I'm including some of them here:
    Codependent No More, by Melodie Beatie
    Healing the Child Within, by Dr. Charles Whitfield
    Homecoming: Reclaiming and Championing Your Inner Child, by John Bradshaw
    Learning to Love Yourself Workbook, by Gay Hendricks Ph.D.
    The Road Less Traveled, by M. Scott Peck, MD
    You Can Heal Your Life, by Louise Hay
    The Journey from Abandonment to Healing, by Susan Anderson

8. If you were sexually abused, I'd recommend *The Courage to Heal*, on female sexual abuse, by Ellen Bass and Laura Davis or *Victims No Longer*, on male sexual abuse, by Mike Lew.

9. Before you finish, please write a few pages about how you feel after doing the homework today. Remember the hot pen technique; just write, write, write! Focus on your feelings as much as you can.

Hey, you're doing great! I'm so proud of you for deciding to face the truth about your life head on! I know sometimes the truth hurts, but trust me; you're going to be so happy that you did it! I can hardly wait to see the changes that will come in your life as you keep on trucking down this road! It's going to be a wonderful, magical experience!

Chapter Three

Develop Your
Emotional Intelligence!

Jan

Jan was born the sixth child in a family of eight. Her mother was kind-hearted but she was overwhelmed with raising so many children. Jan's father, however, was violent and abusive. Jan and her siblings grew up always fearing their father because of his explosive temper. They never knew when his mood would erupt into verbal, physical, emotional or sexual abuse.

Jan's dad would hit Jan and her siblings with 2x4 boards and leave welts and bruises on them regularly. One of her brothers was so traumatized by her father's beatings that he committed suicide later in life. Jan's mother was afraid to divorce her dad because he told her he would kill her if she divorced him. When she finally found the courage to separate, Jan's dad stopped beating Jan and her siblings. He continued the sexual abuse with Jan, however, until they moved across the country and he could no longer reach her.

Jan felt all her life that there was something wrong with her and that she had somehow deserved her father's abusive treatment. When she left home as a young adult, she found friends and partners who also abused her, which validated her belief that she was the problem, not them. Jan struggled to survive her past by using alcohol and cocaine to numb the pain. She became a sexual addict in her desperate search to be loved. She was also anorexic and bulimic at times in an effort to deal with the unbearable pain of her life.

The pain of her life and her choices reached an all-time high when finally a friend intervened one day and invited her to one of my weekend personal growth workshops. Jan says her healing journey started at that workshop. She really hoped that one weekend of personal growth would heal all the pain, but she soon realized it was only the tip of the iceberg.

The first time Jan came to see me individually she was so terrified of facing her true feelings that she didn't come back again for six months. She said she was very afraid of what she would find when she looked inward. Eventually she came back and tried again, and then with continued caring and nurturing over time, she was finally able to face her intense childhood pain.

Jan continued therapy in individual and group sessions for a couple of years. She says she experienced miraculous inner changes when she was able to feel and release the pain of her life in a safe, supportive environment. She learned to cry, scream, and even pound pillows to release the excruciating emotional pain. Then when she felt clearer emotionally, she learned to support that sweet, innocent little girl inside her.

Jan says she categorizes her life as pre-Kari and post-Kari because she sees her life as an example of extreme polar opposites. Through her emotional healing journey, she was able to release all of her addictions. She built a support system of wonderful friends who loved her unconditionally and supported her healing. In time, she also found a loving partner and began working to establish a healthy relationship.

Fortunately Jan was able to work through most of the backlog of the severe emotional pain of her life before she and her husband were blessed with a beautiful baby boy. After the poor role modeling in her childhood, Jan was at first very concerned about being a healthy parent to her new son. With the help and support of her loving husband, however, she feels very happy today to know that she is raising a healthy, happy child. After everything Jan has been through, her life today is definitely an incredible miracle!

Days 5 and 6

Hello again! Welcome back! This is a very important day in your emotional healing journey, because today you're going to learn one of the most valuable lessons in this entire book. You will undoubtedly need to come back to today's lesson over and over, because it's not something you can master in only one session or one day. It's an emotional healing process that you will need to practice again and again to become proficient with it, but over time you'll learn to do it very quickly and easily.

So, are you ready? Great! Today I'm going to teach you the beginning skills for developing your emotional intelligence. Let me explain. I'm sure you're all familiar with the term "IQ" which is your intelligence quotient. We've always understood the importance of intelligence in our culture, but it's only recently that we've also become aware of the importance of our "EQ" or our emotional intelligence.

Daniel Goleman, Ph.D. originally coined the term "emotional intelligence" during the mid 1990s. His enlightening book *Emotional Intelligence, Why It Can Matter More than IQ,* showed that no matter how smart people are intellectually, if they aren't equally capable emotionally, they simply aren't able to fully utilize their intellectual capabilities in their everyday lives. If you think about that concept for a moment, you'll realize how very true it is. Most of us know people who are intellectually brilliant, but emotionally damaged to the point that they simply can't function in their every day lives.

Growing up in dysfunctional families makes it very difficult for us to have a high "EQ" because our parents didn't encourage us to express our feelings or our needs, so we never had the opportunity to learn how to recognize them or express them appropriately. Remember that our parents also came from dysfunctional homes, so they probably didn't know how to teach us about expressing our feelings. Generally they weren't able to role model healthy communication or healthy conflict resolution either. If our dysfunctional families expressed any feelings at all, they were usually expressed inappropriately with arguing and fighting.

Developing emotional intelligence after growing up in a dysfunctional family is a healing journey that happens little by little over time. It requires first of all that you learn to identify and express your feelings and your needs, and secondly that you also learn to resolve them and release them. When you've spent most of your life denying your feelings and needs or expressing them inappropriately, learning to name them accurately and express them honestly can feel overwhelming. You'll need to be very patient and kind with yourself in this process.

Resolving and releasing the feelings can be equally challenging. I'm sure you've heard the term 'catch and release' that fishermen use, especially those who enjoy the process of fishing but don't want to eat the fish they catch. Releasing your feelings is a somewhat similar experience. You'll want to catch and name the feeling, learn what you need to learn from it, and then toss it back into the ocean to be swallowed up in the waves of life. The good news is that by learning to express and release the feelings, you can avoid spending years of your precious life stuck in the pain of what happened in the past.

So let's talk about you. If you were raised in a dysfunctional family, chances are you're not very good at recognizing and naming your feelings. Maybe you know you feel bad, but you don't know what the feeling is or what you can do to release it and feel better. I understand how that feels because I had the same experience years ago. When I first started working through my feelings, my therapist would ask me what I felt, and I had only two words for my feelings. I either felt "good" or I felt "shitty." It was definitely a limited vocabulary, but later, that experience taught me how to help my clients who don't have words learn how to express their emotions more clearly.

I have learned in working with my clients that there are six basic feelings; they are angry, sad, scared, hurt, happy, and peaceful. If you want to learn to recognize your feelings and name them accurately, that process is often like playing detective on yourself. If you feel bad and you didn't know why, you can go down the list and cross off the ones that don't fit. For example, you could say, "Well, I know I'm not happy or peaceful right now, and it doesn't feel like I'm angry or scared, so I must be sad or hurt."

In order to clarify why you are feeling sad or hurt, you can ask yourself "When did this feeling start? Was I feeling sad when I woke up this morning? Was it there at lunch or dinner yesterday?" It's like retracing your steps to find something that you lost; sometimes you have to think about what happened in the last few hours to see when your feelings changed. When you can clarify when the feeling started, then you can ask your self "What was happening around that time? Who was I with? What were we talking about? What was I reading? Did that experience remind me of something in my past?"

When you know when the feeling started, then you have some clues as to what it's about. Then you can ask yourself to finish the sentence "I'm sad that…" or "It hurts me that…" and see what comes to your mind. Don't ever worry about having the wrong answer with feelings. Feelings are like water; they can change directions or wash away in a moment. There aren't any right or wrong answers with feelings. You just have to start somewhere and then let them grow or change along the way.

There are a couple of things you will want to avoid in working with your feelings. One thing to avoid is believing that a feeling you have about yourself is the truth about you. For example, if you feel 'less than' a friend of yours, it's important to remember that the feeling of being 'less than' your friend is just a feeling. It's not the truth about you. *Feelings are not the truth, they're just there to resolve and release.*

The other thing you'll want to avoid is believing that your feeling about someone else is the truth about that person. Just because you feel hurt by something someone has said or done, doesn't mean that person has really "done you wrong." When you feel and release the feeling, you may find that the person who hurt you in the present was only the trigger for a deeper feeling you need to resolve and release from the past. When you resolve and release the old feeling, you will probably see the present situation much differently.

In working with my clients, I learned that specific feelings relate to tension in specific parts of the body. For example, when your back or your arms are tense or tight, you are often angry or frustrated about something. If your chest is tight or tense, you are generally hurt or sad. When your stomach is tight, it's often related to being angry or scared. (If you pay attention over time, you'll learn to distinguish whether the tension in your stomach is from being angry or from being scared, because the feeling is different.) When your body is completely relaxed and you have an overall feeling of well being, you are happy or peaceful.

In order to resolve and release your feelings, you have to let yourself really feel them and express them in some way. Sometimes just writing about what you feel in your journal will be enough to help you understand the feelings and let go of them. Sometimes you will need to talk with another human being who can listen and care about what you are feeling, so that you feel validated and understood.

It's important to know that feelings are not just in our minds, they have a distinct physical energy in our bodies. Sometimes just talking is not enough and you need to express your hurt by crying, or release your anger by pounding on a pillow to release the physical energy from your body. Sometimes we have to physically release our feelings by working out, or running, or doing some other type of physical exercise so that our physical bodies feel relieved. When we physically feel lighter and freer, then we can move on to being that lighthearted, happy person we want to be.

Releasing your feelings does not need to involve talking directly to the person who upset you. In fact, often it's a good idea not to talk directly to that person, especially if your feelings are strong or intense. When you first begin releasing your feelings, the backlog of anger and hurt can be intense and overwhelming, because you've been holding it inside for a lifetime. As you continue resolving and releasing the feelings over time, they generally become easier and less intense.

Keep in mind that releasing your feelings is for your own benefit right now, not anyone else's. Later in this book, when you've released the original intensity of your emotional pain and you can talk more calmly, I'll teach you how to express your feelings appropriately and nonviolently to the people who matter most to you. For now, just do this emotional healing work for your own benefit.

So, would you like to give this process a try? Okay, let's try an example. Let's say you notice that you have a feeling of heaviness in your chest. When you go through the list above, you realize that heaviness in your chest often relates to feeling sad or hurt. Between sadness and hurt, you may feel that sadness fits the feeling inside you better than hurt in this particular case, but when you try to answer the sentence "I'm sad that…" you may not know immediately what you're feeling sad about.

You may have to play detective on yourself at this point, by going back over the past twenty-four hours and asking yourself when this feeling began. Perhaps you find that the heaviness in your chest started near the time a friend told you about an exciting promotion they were getting on their job. So even though you are truly happy about your friend's promotion, maybe a part of you is sad that you haven't been promoted in you own career.

When you can name your feeling and understand why you feel the way you do, you can do something to resolve it. With this example of your friend's promotion and the sadness about your own career not moving forward, you could express the sadness by talking to someone you trust about it or by writing in your journal. Using the sentence "I'm sad that" you might say "I'm sad that no one values or appreciates the long hours I spend at work," or "I'm sad that I haven't been recognized for my talents or abilities," "I'm sad that no matter how hard I try, someone else always does it better."

Many times a feeling in the present connects to an old feeling from childhood. When that happens, it's not so much the situation in the present that upsets you but what it reminds you of in the past. In this situation, when you feel your sadness about not being promoted, you may find that it triggers old feelings from when you were a child. Maybe your father never acknowledged your efforts or your successes as a child.

If you want to really get to the root of your sadness, you'll have to let yourself feel how it felt to never be able to please your dad as a child.

You could write a letter to your dad and tell him what you're feeling. You're not going to send the letter (in fact you may want to burn it when it's done), so you can say anything you want in this letter for now. Remember the purpose of writing it is not to actually communicate with your dad; it's just to release the feeling.

In your letter you might say "Dear Dad, It really hurt me when you always ignored me when I was a kid. Why didn't you spend time with me and make me feel like I mattered to you? Didn't you see how hard I worked to get you to notice me? When you never noticed my efforts, I got angry and I just gave up on myself. For years I didn't try at all because of you.

Now when I try to work hard to catch up with other people my age, it still brings up those old feelings of anger and hurt and sadness, because it feels like no matter what I do, no one will ever notice it or acknowledge it. Why couldn't you take the time to love me and notice me back then? It still hurts me even today, Dad. I don't know if I'll ever be able to be the person I want to be!"

You may need to cry while you're writing, or you may need to get angry and pound on a punching bag to really release the feeling, but when it's released, you'll feel stronger and lighter inside. It's an amazing process, but when you try it you'll see that it really does work. It's very freeing to finally let go of that bag of bricks you've been carrying on you back!

So we have one more thing to discuss before we complete today. You're going to enjoy this part. A very core issue we have with growing up in dysfunctional families is that too often we didn't get our feelings and needs validated. We didn't get the nurturing and comfort we needed when we did try to express what we felt. Often our parents didn't realize that we needed to be hugged and comforted and that we needed to hear positive, reassuring words to replace the negative ones.

Because of that lack of nurturing and comfort, it's important to remember that when you have released your negative feelings, you will also need to fill that empty space you've created with positive, loving words and images for the little child inside you. One way to do that is to imagine yourself as an adult walking into your life as a child and loving that little boy or girl like he or she was your own son or daughter.

It's very healing to imagine holding that little child in your arms and saying loving, healing words to him or her. When you imagine holding your inner child you might say loving words like "I love you just the way you are," or "You're very special and important to me," or "No matter what happens, I'm always going to be there for you!"

It's also very fun to imagine taking your inner child out to play and imagine doing the things you wish you could have done as a child. Maybe you'd enjoy taking your inner child to the park to play, or maybe you'd like to fly a kite together. Maybe you'll want to go for a walk in the woods or build a sand castle. We'll practice playing with your inner child today in your homework, so you'll get the feeling of what I'm talking about, okay?

So in conclusion for today, I'd like you to remember that feelings are just feelings. They don't have to control you long-term. There is always a way to release them if you want to. You just have to be diligent and persistent in your intention to identify, resolve and release them. Some feelings take more time to release than others, but there is always a way to get through them if you are determined.

The purpose of resolving and releasing your feelings is to let go of the effects of growing up in a dysfunctional family and become the person you were meant to be in the world. *Every time you resolve and release a feeling, you are one step closer to being that bright, shining spirit you were meant to be.* Your emotional intelligence will soar to new heights as you grow and expand into your truest self.

I have a very important secret I want to share with you today before we finish. I hope you'll take it to heart and memorize it for a lifetime. *The secret is that all feelings when expressed and released come back to peace and love.* So, when you do the emotional work it takes to resolve and release your feelings, the unconditional love you have for yourself and others is the payoff for all your time and effort.

So let's practice! We'll start your homework today with getting in touch with what you are feeling right now. To express and release your feelings, you have to always start with the feeling you have in this particular moment and then, if necessary, you can trace it back to where it originated in childhood. Please get your journal and let's get started. Are you ready?

Homework Assignment: Chapter Three

1. Start a new page in your journal and write at the top of the page "Identifying and releasing my feelings."

2. It's a good idea to start this process by taking at least ten big deep breaths to help you get in touch with the feelings in your body, and remember to continue breathing deeply throughout the process. *Breathing deeply helps you release the feelings from your body, not just your mind.*

3. I'd like you to write in your journal the six basic feelings; angry sad, scared, hurt, happy, peaceful. Now ask yourself, "Which feeling is the strongest for me right now in this moment?" Are you angry? Are you scared? Are you sad? Are you hurt? Are you happy? Are you peaceful? Maybe you have several feelings at once. If so, write them all down.

4. Now, check in with your body. Is there tension in your body right now? Where is the tension? Is it in your stomach? Is it in your chest? Is it in your arms, your shoulders, or your back? *Remember that your stomach often has to do with anger or fear, chest is often hurt or sad, and arms and shoulders and back are often about anger, resentment or frustration.* Please write which part of your body is tense or tight and whether the feeling coincides with the feeling you thought was most prevalent.

5. Now, beginning with your strongest feeling, please write "I'm angry that..." or "It hurts me that..." and finish the sentence with whatever comes to your mind. It's a good idea to finish the sentence at least 3 times with 3 different answers, and then ask yourself which one do you feel the most strongly.

In the same way, if the feeling is sadness or fear, write "I'm sad that…" or "I'm scared that…" and finish the sentence three different ways, asking yourself at the end which of the three is the strongest feeling for you right now. For example, you might say, "I'm sad that I'm alone. I'm sad that my partner left me. I'm sad that my kids don't want to see me." Then ask yourself which of these feelings is the strongest. Maybe the feeling of your partner leaving is the one that really hurts the most right now.

6. Now take the strongest feeling you have right now and think of whom that feeling relates to in your life. Is it your husband, your wife, your mother, or your father? Maybe it's your son, or your daughter, or your boss at work. If you could tell this person what you are feeling, and you didn't have to worry about their feelings or their response, what would you say?

   Write your feelings in your journal using their first name, just like you'd say it them to them in person, starting with "Mary, I'm really angry that…" or "John, it really hurts me that…" or "Bill, I'm scared that…" Be clear and specific and keep writing till you feel some relief, like "Wow, that's what I have needed to say all this time!"

   You can say anything you want to say in your journal, but please don't go talk to them in person at this point. We have more work to do before you are ready to do that!

7. Does the feeling you have in the present remind you of feelings in the past? If you are angry or hurt by your partner or by a friend today, ask yourself when you felt this anger or hurt before in your life. Did you feel the same feelings with your Mom or Dad as a child, or with an early caregiver? What do you still need to say to that person who hurt you in childhood?

   Write your feelings again, focusing on your Mom or Dad or whomever caused those feelings in the past, and be very clear and emphatic in what you say. You may need to say something like this: "Mom, it really hurt me when you didn't protect me from Dad! I was just a little child and I needed your love and protection. Because of what happened back then, it's still hard for me to trust that people will be there for me!"

Remember that it's not a good idea to talk to anyone in person at this point. This process is for healing you and releasing your feelings. We'll deal with your relationships with others later.

8. If you have more than one strong feeling going on in this moment, please repeat #6 and #7 with each feeling.

9. The reason for getting in touch with the feeling is simply to be able to name it and feel it totally, then express it and release it so that you can come back to the love and peace inside. There's no point in staying stuck in the pain any longer than it takes to name it, feel it, express it and release it!

    If you're not feeling a release from the feeling, please write in your journal about what you could do without hurting anyone to release this feeling. Would it help to cry? Would it help to get outside and exercise? Sometimes walking or running helps to release the feeling. Could you talk to someone you trust about the feeling without hurting anyone? If you are angry, would it help you to pound some pillows or get some physical exercise to release the anger?

    Remember that it's never okay to hurt someone with your anger. What we're doing is simply learning how to release the feeling and let it go, so that you can come back to that incredible feeling of love and peace inside you. Trust me; you'll absolutely love it when you get there!

10. When you believe that you have successfully released the feeling, check inside your body and notice if there is any part that still feels tense or tight. *Tension is a signal that you're not complete. When you have truly released the feeling, your body should be totally relaxed and you should be feeling a sense of relief.* If you don't feel relief, it's because the feeling has not been released, so go back and do the process again until you honestly feel better.

11. When you are complete and your body is free of tension, I want you to find a comfortable place to sit down and relax, in a safe place where you won't be disturbed. If you're in your house, please lock your doors, turn off your phones, put on some soft music, light a candle, or burn your favorite incense.

A. Read through this exercise a couple of times and then sit down and close your eyes and relax deeply while you do the process. If you want to really enjoy the relaxation, start at the top of your head and relax each part of your body slowly till you get to the soles of your feet.

B. I want you to imagine the grown-up part of you, or your adult self, walking into the life of the child you were, your inner child, and loving that child the way you needed to be loved back then. How would you love that little person today? How would you show them that they are important to you and that their feelings do matter? Would you hug him or her, or hold him/her on your lap and talk to them?

C. What loving words would you say to your inner child? What words did you always want to hear as a child? Maybe you would want to say, "I love you just the way you are! You're very important to me. I'm very sorry you were hurt! Nobody knows better than me what it was like for you growing up! From now on, I'm going to be here for you. We're going to get through this together!"

D. Take a few moments to play with your inner child. Ask your inner child what he or she would like to do. Then imagine playing in the park together, or building a sand castle, or flying a kite, or laughing together till you wet your pants like you did when you were young and free.

E. When you're feeling complete, take a little time to bring your awareness back to the present. Take some big deep breaths and wiggle your fingers and toes. When you're ready, you can open your eyes.

12. When you have finished the process, please write a few pages in your journal about what you experienced today and how it felt.

13. If you'd like to read about the importance of emotional healing, I'd suggest a couple of books:
    Emotional Intelligence by Daniel Goleman, Ph.D.
    Molecules of Emotion by Candace Pert Ph.D.

Congratulations! You did great today! I know that this is very hard work, but if you come back to it and make it a part of your everyday life, this emotional healing process will change your life forever. Remember that you will need to come back to today's homework over and over; it's not a one-time thing. It's an amazing inner journey that will help you learn to deal with your life totally differently than you've ever done before. When you learn to feel and release your feelings and love the child inside you regularly, in time you will honestly feel like a whole new person!

Chapter Four

Understand Your Unconscious Mind and Give Up The Drama!

Annette

Annette's life before emotional healing was full of drama! She was born the middle daughter in a family of six children. Annette describes her Dad as strong, out-going, opinionated and boisterous, while her Mom was gentle and loving, but silently angry. Annette's family moved fourteen times during her childhood, often because they didn't have money to pay the rent.

Annette has little memory of her childhood, except that her Dad was always gone and when he was home her parents were always drinking. Annette remembers her childhood as filled with miserable fighting between her siblings with never any resolution. There was no emotional guidance and no positive discipline in her family. Annette felt no joy and had no sense of herself as a person.

When she was in high school the phone rang one day and a stranger on the phone said that he was her brother. He and another brother showed up later that day at her house. They looked identical to her Dad and Annette found out later that day that her father also had another family of six before he married her mother.

When Annette was eighteen, her father was diagnosed with

three kinds of cancer. Annette had just been awarded a scholarship for being the most promising teacher in the state and had already signed up to go to college when she was the one chosen to be her Dad's caregiver. For three months while he lay dying, Annette listened to her Dad scream in pain and hallucinate about his dysfunctional life. Annette understood her father's intense pain later in life when she found out that her that he had sexually abused his sisters and his daughters from his first marriage.

When her father died Annette did go to college briefly, but after a time she and a friend decided to become Catholic nuns. Annette tried out her new calling by living in a convent that summer. While she was there she became a representative from the convent to the local parish counsel.

Annette met an interesting man at her first parish counsel meeting. Although he was married and she was preparing to be a nun, she fell madly in love with him. Within a month, his wife and two children died in a house fire. Annette and her new love began meeting soon after the funeral of his wife and children. Within only eighteen months, they were married and their son was born. Annette was happy in the marriage for a time, but five years later her husband became ill and died of leukemia. Annette realizes now that she had never let him grieve the loss of his family.

Annette became very depressed after the death of her husband. For two years she drank steadily to numb her pain. She met her current husband in a bar and they continued drinking together. When I first met Annette, she was facing the third death of someone she loved. She was caring for her dying mother and still numbing her pain with alcohol. Annette came to one of my weekend workshops that summer and began her healing journey.

Annette says that emotional healing introduced her to the world of feelings. She says finally she felt like she was 'someone.' She came to realize that her feelings and needs were important. She was granted permission to feel the emotions in her body and taught ways to deal with those feelings in appropriate ways. It was a relief to finally realize that she wasn't wrong. She just needed to tools to get the feelings out and release them.

Today Annette helps others heal in her career as a life coach. She also provides incredibly beautiful heart-felt ceremonies for weddings and funerals and other important life celebrations. Annette says the answers to life's ups and downs come through with crystal clarity when a person stays in touch with their feelings and releases them regularly. Annette doesn't suppress her tears or her laughter anymore. She feels free to do, say, or feel whatever is real in the moment and she believes that helps her travel to the next moment without emotional baggage. Annette says energy when used appropriately creates miracles. She is truly a miracle!

Days 7 and 8

Hi there! How are you today? Does working through your feelings seem like hard work to you? Are you feeling like you want to give up and do something that's not so scary or so challenging? Don't worry! It's normal to feel like that. Why do you think you've avoided your feelings for so long? Obviously you were a little scared of facing your feelings or you would have done it a long time ago, right?

You see, back when you were a little boy or a little girl, you probably didn't have the love and support you needed when difficult things came up in your life. Like we said before, your parents may have had the best intentions in the world, but they simply didn't understand what you needed, or didn't see the value of helping you resolve things. Even if they were good people, they probably never learned how to deal with their own feelings, let alone know how to help you with yours!

If you had toxic parents who were intentionally abusive or neglectful, then it's probably even scarier for you to think about what you feel, because you may have felt physically or emotionally in danger as a child if you even mentioned what you felt. Some of you may remember the line some parents used which was "If you don't stop crying, I'll give you something to cry about!" I sincerely hope you didn't have that kind of parent, but if you did, you can still heal the emotional pain. I've helped many people who came from extremely abusive situations heal the past and get on with making their life better. You can do it too, even if you're shaking in your shoes right now. Don't worry! We'll get you there!

If you feel like you need a real person right now and not just a book to support you in this process, please feel free to call a friend, call the mental health hotline in your area or call a mental health professional and schedule a time to talk to someone personally. Sometimes it really helps just to feel like somebody cares and somebody understands the pain you've been through.

Emotions are hard work! Healing the emotional pain from the past is not a job for sissies or for wimps. It's a "Roll up your sleeves and shovel horse manure" kind of job, if you know what I mean! It takes a lot of courage to face your issues and resolve them, but it's not impossible. You can do it, if you want to!

So today we're going to talk about how to give up the drama in your life and start facing the real issues. In order to do that it's important to understand your unconscious mind and know how it works. Remember what they taught you in grade school that everybody has both a conscious mind and an unconscious mind? We're going to go a bit beyond that today, so let me refresh your memory a bit.

The conscious mind is the logical, practical side of you that goes to work and gets things done. It's the part of your mind you are generally using in your day-to-day activities. Your conscious mind gets you to work in the morning, helps you accomplish your tasks on the job, and helps you organize your life and pay your bills at home.

The unconscious mind, on the other hand, is the part of your mind that stores old memories and feelings from the past. It's the emotional, creative or passionate side of you that stays in the background in your everyday world. Your unconscious mind has a way of coming up when you least expect it to create either beauty or havoc in your life, depending on what you've stored in your unconscious files.

Let me explain how your unconscious mind works. Your unconscious mind is filled with the experiences and memories and feelings of your past. If you had lots of happy, positive experiences in your life, and if when you had experiences that were difficult or painful, there were people available to love you and support you, then you probably have a happy, fully functioning life today.

If, on the other hand, you had a lot of unhappy experiences in your life and there was no one around to help you work though the painful feelings from those experiences, then you probably have a lot of painful, unresolved feelings stored in your unconscious mind. If that is true, those unresolved feelings are undoubtedly still festering in your unconscious mind and still causing you emotional pain today. That's what growing up in dysfunctional families is all about.

But here's the catch! Please pay attention to this. There's another part of your mind, let's call it your super-conscious mind, that is always trying to help you heal whatever is unresolved in your unconscious mind. *The way it helps you heal is by creating situations that repeat the unresolved feelings from the past over and over in your life so that you can have another opportunity to heal the emotional pain.* In other words, your super-conscious mind gives you the same old feelings to deal with in new situations, over and over again, until you finally express and release those feelings and learn whatever it is that you need to learn from them.

You might be asking why the super-conscious mind thinks this is helping you and what you could possibly need to learn from those old painful, unresolved feelings. Good question! Take a big, deep breath and try to really think about what I'm saying to you. The lessons your super-conscious mind wants you to learn from feeling and releasing the unresolved pain from the past are always about you loving yourself unconditionally and becoming the person you were meant to be on the earth. Isn't that incredible?

It may surprise you to know that all those difficult situations in your life were actually meant to help you learn to love yourself unconditionally and become the person you were meant to be in the world. I understand. I know it's hard to believe, but it's true. Your super-conscious mind actually wants the best for you. It's honestly trying to help you by giving you new opportunities every day to learn whatever you need to learn about self-acceptance, self-love, and self-actualization!

If I were you, I'd probably be asking how a person is supposed to learn about loving themselves in the middle of all that drama and trauma. That's a million-dollar question, isn't it? How are you supposed to learn lessons about unconditional love and self-actualization when you're hurting, or angry, or scared?

Okay, let's try giving you an example and see if that helps you understand. Let's say your partner or a friend of yours said something that really hurt you today. Maybe you're feeling hurt and angry or even a little revengeful, like you want to hurt them back so that they will know how it feels. Those feelings of wanting to get even are totally normal for a child, but now that you're an adult, you may want to consider a healthier, more mature approach.

You see, you have a very important choice to make in this situation. You could spend your time being angry and hurt and trying to get revenge, but if you are feeling motivated and courageous, you could attempt a healthier approach. Instead of continuing the drama and trying to get even with them, you could choose to feel and release the hurt and anger, like we talked about in yesterday's lesson, and then take it a step further and try to understand what your super-conscious mind is trying to teach you.

If you want to really understand the lesson your super-conscious mind wants you to learn, you may need to ask yourself, "What does this situation remind me of in my past?" Maybe what the person said today that felt hurtful is similar to something your Mom or Dad said to you when you were young.

So along with telling this person in the present how you feel, when you do your feeling and releasing homework, you may also need to tell your Mom or Dad how it felt when they hurt you as a child. You may have to think of different ways to say what you feel, until what you're saying really hits the spot inside.

Just keep writing in your journal about your feelings until the feelings actually release and you feel clearer and stronger. Don't forget that when you've released the feelings, it's always good to spend some time loving the child inside you like you wish you would have been loved back then.

When that process is all done and you're feeling calm and peaceful inside, you could say to yourself "I wonder what I have to learn from this situation?" The lesson you need to learn is always some version of the real truth about you as a person. The real truth is that you were actually a valuable, beautiful child who deserved to be treated with love and respect whether or not your parents were able to provide that for you.

So the person who said something that hurt you in the present was actually giving you a gift by making you aware of something in your unconscious mind that needed healing. I know it doesn't feel like a gift, but the good news is when you really learn the lesson you need to learn from this situation, you will actually feel deep inside yourself that you are lovable and valuable. When that happens, your super-conscious mind will no longer need to create new situations for you to learn that lesson.

Maybe you're saying, "Okay, okay! I've had enough lessons! Isn't there an easier way to learn?" I know how you feel. Sometimes it does seem a little overwhelming, doesn't it? Not only do we have to go through that hurt and pain the first time, but we also have to repeat it again and again till we get the point. It can definitely be a little frustrating!

But now we get to the good part! The second million-dollar question is this; now that you finally understand what your unconscious mind is doing, how can knowing that help you to stop creating the drama in your life?

Well, it's a lot like letting the air out of a big balloon. *When you don't buy into the drama, the drama simply loses its hold on you.* When you say to yourself, "There's something I need to learn from this" instead of fighting, and blaming, and attacking the person who hurt you, then it sets you both free to use your emotional energy in more positive, efficient ways.

Are you wondering if everyone in your present life that is hurting you or making you angry is actually giving you an emotional gift? Brace yourself, because the answer is "Yes!" Everyone in your present life who brings up those painful feelings in you is actually helping you get in touch with the unresolved feelings from the past. When you feel and release those old, unresolved feelings, you will finally get it at a gut level that you are truly beautiful and lovable and that you really deserve to be treated with love and respect every day of your life.

Before we complete today, let's talk about what happens when we don't work through our feelings from the past. I'm sure you see examples of people who are not working through their feelings every day, because they're everywhere around us every day. Remember that when we choose not to deal with our feelings, our feelings have to go somewhere. Feelings have energy and energy has to be expressed somehow. It doesn't just disappear.

What happens when we're not dealing directly and appropriately with our feelings is that we either act them 'in' on ourselves, or we act them 'out' on other people. When we act them 'in' on ourselves, we become anxious, depressed and withdrawn, and we blame ourselves for everything around us that goes wrong. When we act our feelings 'out' on other people, we become angry and abusive, and we blame everyone around us for our problems.

All of the negative behaviors you see in people around you in your life are the result of someone not dealing with their feelings in healthy, appropriate ways. When people are angry, disrespectful, uncaring or abusive, you can be sure that they have painful feelings inside that they haven't dealt with appropriately. Many times they are still denying their emotional pain, which forces that pain to come out in unhealthy ways. The same is true of people who are depressed and withdrawn. They undoubtedly have a reservoir of unresolved feelings from the past that need to be healed.

Keep in mind that if you have negative behaviors that make your life difficult, those behaviors are the result of you not dealing with your own feelings. Maybe you didn't even realize that your past was affecting you, but obviously it has if the negative behaviors are there. The good news is that when you choose to face that emotional pain and deal with it directly and appropriately, your negative behaviors will change naturally. You'll be able to actually feel proud of who you are as a person! Isn't that an exciting thought?

So your emotional healing journey throughout this book will involve feeling, expressing, and healing your unresolved feelings from the past.

If you want to be happy and lighthearted, you'll need to grow emotionally to the point where you don't have to fight with anyone because there's really nothing to fight about anymore.

When you get to that point of inner peace and unconditional love, you will also know your own value and worth from the inside out. You will simply no longer accept anything less than love and respect in your life, because you will know in every cell of your body that you are beautiful and lovable and that you absolutely deserve to be treated with love and respect.

So that's what I want you to focus on today and tomorrow, as you are doing your homework assignment. How can you stop buying in to the drama of your life and start utilizing your emotional energy in more positive ways? Are you ready to get to work? I am. Let's get started!

Homework Assignment: Chapter Four

1. I'd like for you to think about some feelings that have come up for you again and again in your life. Write a paragraph or two about any pattern you see in your life where your unconscious mind is recreating similar situations that bring up the same feelings again and again.

2. Now, take the most recent experience where you felt the feeling, and go back and do yesterday's homework focused on it. I'd like you to express and release this feeling by writing about it in your journal until you come back to the feeling of peace and calm inside. Remember when it's complete that you need to love, support and nurture your inner child and spend some time playing with him or her.

3. When that is complete, ask yourself "What is my unconscious mind trying to help me learn about myself from this experience?" What is the real truth of who I am that I didn't realize before? Remember the real truth is always some version of the thought that you are a valuable, beautiful person who absolutely deserves to be treated

with love and respect, whether or not your parents were able to provide that for you as a child.

4.   Now, think about how you could spend your valuable time and your precious emotional energy if you were not buying into the drama of your life, and write about what you would like to do with that valuable time and energy instead.

5.   There are many books that might be helpful to you in this process. Go to the library or to a bookstore near you and browse in the psychology or self-help section if you feel like you need more information. Ask your angel guides to help you find the book that's perfect for you right now. Often when you do that the perfect book will just jump off the shelf at you!

6.   Here are some books that I would recommend for those of you who came from severely abusive homes:
Toxic Parents, Overcoming Their Hurtful Legacy and Reclaiming Your Life, by Susan Forward.
The Family, by John Bradshaw
Healing the Shame that Binds You, by John Bradshaw
I Don't Want To Talk About It, a book on male depression by Terrance Real
Adult Children of Abusive Parents, by Steven Farmer, MA

7.   Write a few pages in your journal about how you feel after doing today's homework. Remember just to write, write, write!

Good job! I'm so proud of you! Learning to give up the drama of your life and choosing instead to use your energy positively will turn your whole life around. Wow! You're going to be so excited when you see it happening!

Chapter Five

Change Your Thoughts, Change Your Beliefs and Change Your Life!

Sarah

Sarah was only sixteen years old when she found my website on the Internet. She wrote me an e-mail asking if I knew of any psychotherapists in her area who focused on sexual abuse issues. Sarah lived thousands of miles from my psychotherapy practice, so it was a difficult question to answer. Her e-mail said that that she had already been to many therapists and hospitals in her young life and none of them had helped.

Sarah and I began writing daily e-mail correspondence. When we first began writing, Sarah was extremely depressed and often suicidal. She told me her father was in jail for raping a fourteen-year-old girl in their town. He had also raped and abused Sarah and her sisters before they were five years old.

Sarah had dropped out of school in the eighth grade. She had no friends her own age, because she didn't think anyone would want to be around her. She spent most of her time locked up in her bedroom in the dark, either writing in sexual abuse chat rooms or watching Disney movies to escape the pain. When the emotional pain got too intense, Sarah would cut gashes in her arms to relieve it.

As we continued writing, I learned that Sarah had also been raped and abused by several other men in her town. After being victimized as a child, Sarah had no emotional skills for defending herself from abusers. She reported feeling terrified and paralyzed in abusive situations, not knowing what to do to protect herself. Later I learned that an older neighborhood man was still sexually abusing Sarah several times a week while we were corresponding, but she didn't tell me that at the time.

After nine months, Sarah convinced her mother to let her fly to Spokane to attend one of my weekend personal growth workshops. She had never been away from home and never flown on a commercial airplane, but she wanted to get better so badly that she was willing to fly across the country by herself and be in a group of total strangers. I was shocked and amazed at her courage!

Sarah hardly spoke all weekend that first time she came, just watching wide-eyed while other people in the group shared their emotional pain. Later she told us that she had never experienced anything like what she was witnessing in the group. Her family at home was alcoholic, and her aunts and uncles were verbally and physically abusive whenever they got together. No one was ever intentionally vulnerable and no one shared their authentic feelings with each other unless they were drunk.

By the time Sarah came back for her second personal growth workshop, she had bonded emotionally with other workshop participants. One of them invited her to stay in our area to start a new life for her self. Sarah had a very difficult time believing that her life could get better, but with the support of a loving community, she got her GED and enrolled in community college. At the end of the first college term she was on the honor role, much to everyone's amazement and surprise!

Sarah is presently completing her second year of college.

What has challenged her most on her emotional healing journey has been working to change her negative thoughts and beliefs. With a history like hers, it has taken a very concerted effort on her part to believe that she is valuable and that people do love her and sincerely want to support her.

Sarah told me recently that she feels very proud of herself, because she overcame a huge hurdle in her life. She went back to visit her family last month and even though things had not changed back there, she was able to tell herself while she was there that she was okay and that life would get better. Sarah said that she did not resort to cutting on her arms like she used to when she was hurting and she never even once contemplated suicide!

Days 9 and 10

Hello again! How are you doing? I hope you're enjoying this process as much as I am. The good news is that you will enjoy it more and more as you keep traveling down this path. When you see the payoff for all your hard work, it is definitely worth every moment you put into it!

I was lucky to start my growth process in my early twenties. We were really fishing in the dark in those days, trying to find the solutions to what was wrong with us, because the information we have now about emotional and psychological healing simply wasn't available. Like we talked about before, back then we had to 'invent the wheel' in almost every situation.

Emotional healing was a very long and arduous process for me, compared to how quickly I can teach it to my clients now, and yet, I wouldn't trade it for the world! I'd do it all over again if necessary, because every minute I spent on my growth was well worth it to me. When I look at where my life was when I first started personal growth compared to where it is now, it's literally like the contrast between living in hell or living in heaven. The difference is truly incredible!

You know how much money, time, and energy we spend on buying houses, and cars, and furniture, and trying to look right, or trying to do what other people are doing, or trying to have fun? Yet, too often we still feel empty, and sad and alone underneath the mask that we wear to the world.

But when someone suggests that we spend a little time and money on changing ourselves, or changing our approach to life, we quickly find excuses about how we just can't afford it, or we're just too busy, or we just couldn't possibly do what they are suggesting. We can come up with all kinds of crazy reasons, but they're really just excuses. The question is do you want to get to be fifty or sixty or seventy years old and still feel the way you've felt up till now? Or do you want to learn how to be happy and lighthearted?

Okay, I'll get off my 'soap-box' for now. Let's get busy! Yesterday we talked about learning the lessons that your super-conscious mind is always giving you another opportunity to learn. I hope you still remember that those lessons are always about really getting it at a gut level that you are a special, wonderful human being who absolutely deserves to be treated with love and respect!

Today we're going to take it a step further. The lessons that your super-conscious mind is always trying to teach you are actually about changing the negative beliefs about yourself that you took on from your childhood experiences. When you hold beliefs in your mind that say you are not valuable or not lovable, it has a powerful negative effect on your unconscious mind, and therefore, it also has a powerful negative effect on your life.

The way it works is that your unconscious mind is like a little computer. Whatever you program into the computer of your mind is what you get out. If you program your mind positively, you get positive results, but if you program it negatively, you get negative results. So if you want to have a life that works positively, it's very important to uncover all those negative thoughts and beliefs you took on from childhood and change them to positive thoughts and beliefs.

If you believe, for example, that you are intelligent and creative and that you can do whatever you set your mind to, you will be happy and successful in the world. But if you believe that you're stupid and worthless, and that life always lets you down no matter how hard you try, you'll find yourself always in a pickle, trying to climb your way out of the pickle jar. It's no fun living that way. It's heavy, and ugly, and nobody enjoys it.

As you learned in yesterday's lesson, when your feelings were not honored and your needs were not met in childhood, your normal response is to internalize negative thoughts and beliefs about yourself and about life. Children think the world revolves around them. If your parents treated you with love and respect every day, you probably thought it was because you are so special and important. If they treated you poorly, you thought it was because you are so bad and worthless. Intellectually, you may know as an adult that those negative beliefs you took on are not true, but if your life isn't working the way you want it to, there's definitely a part of you that still believes them.

So here's the secret for today. *You can actually speed up your healing journey by consciously choosing to uncover the negative thoughts and beliefs that you are still carrying and changing them to positive ones.* You'll have to spend some time reprogramming your unconscious mind, but it will save you years of having to learn everything the long, hard way. You'll just have to learn to pay attention to your negative thoughts and change them to positive ones daily. You'll also need to take the time to dig up your old negative beliefs and release them, and then reprogram your unconscious mind with positive beliefs.

So maybe you're wondering what could be some of the typical negative thoughts and beliefs you might have if you grew up in a dysfunctional family? Great! Then let's get to work! There are two types of thoughts and beliefs that need to be changed; one type is the thoughts and beliefs you took on about yourself and the other is the thoughts and beliefs you took on about life itself.

Some of the negative thoughts we often carry into adulthood with us if our parents were not loving and supportive are "I am not good enough to be loved," or "I am not good enough to get what I want." Following closely behind the 'not good enough' thought is the belief that we're 'not worthy' of good things, or that we 'don't deserve' to be treated with love and respect. Children from dysfunctional families often tell themselves that they are stupid, or incompetent, or somehow not capable of success in their lives.

When it comes to life itself, children who experienced a lot of pain and trauma at a young age generally expect that life will bring them more pain and trauma. They often think that that is just the way life is and that there's nothing they can do about it. Because of their history, they simply expect that the negative experiences of the past will be repeated.

Often what I see in my psychotherapy sessions is that my clients take their fears about the future, which come from those negative experiences of the past, and state them like they are the truth about the present. For example a woman might say "I know my husband doesn't really love me," when actually the truth is that she's afraid her husband doesn't care. Or a man might say "I'll never be able to accomplish that because I just don't have what it takes," when actually he's afraid of trying and failing.

If this is something that you do, please be aware that it's a very dangerous habit for your unconscious mind! *Whatever you state as a truth becomes a belief that you carry, and your unconscious mind accepts that belief and goes to work to bring it about in your life.*

Years ago, someone told me that God always says, "Yes" to you. If you believe that life is good and good things will come to you, God says, "Yes," and those beliefs will come true! If you believe, however, that life is terrible and everyone is out to get you, God says "Yes," and your life will be just what you expected! God always says "Yes" to you! So if you want your life to change, you have to look at your every day thoughts and beliefs and start reprogramming your unconscious mind.

No one can change your thoughts and beliefs but you. Other people can help you and support you in this process, but you have to be willing to spend the time and energy delving into your own unconscious mind. The good news is that you can choose at any moment to change your thoughts and beliefs if you are committed and persistent, even starting today!

There are many things you can do to begin reprogramming your mind. We're going to practice some of them today in your homework exercises. You're going to have a chance to really look at your deeply entrenched, negative beliefs about yourself and about life and change them to positive beliefs. I know some powerful ways to help you reprogram the new positive beliefs into your unconscious mind. It's going to be fun!

Along with changing your beliefs, something you can do every day is just make an effort to change negative thoughts you have during the day to positive thoughts. For example, if you hear yourself saying, "This is a rotten day! Nothing is going right!" change it to "It's a little challenging today, but I'm sure it will get better!"

Another good practice for changing your old, negative way of thinking is to take time before you go to bed at night and write three successes you had that day, three things you're thankful for, and three desires you have for things you want to bring into you life in the future. I did that myself for a few months when I was working on reprogramming my unconscious mind and it was very powerful for me.

You see, it's very important to pull out those faulty thoughts and beliefs and change them, unless you want your life to continue playing out just the way it has in the past. *If you don't take the time to reprogram your mind, it will be like replaying an old movie, with the same theme but with different actors, over and over again throughout your life until the day you die.*

So what do you really want? Are you happy with the way your life is working right now? Are you ready to get started changing that old programming? Okay, then let's get to work!

Homework Assignment: Chapter Five

1. Find a clean sheet of paper in your journal, and make a list of the 10 most negative beliefs you have about yourself and your life. For example, your list might read like this:

    1. I'm not good enough.
    2. I don't deserve to be loved.
    3. I always choose men or women who use or abuse me.
    4. I'm a failure.
    5. No one wants to be around me.
    6. I'm stupid, or I'm not smart enough to succeed in life.
    7. Everything I try goes to hell.

8. Life is difficult.

9. Nothing ever gets better.

10. I'll never find the happiness I'm looking for.

2. Okay, you're doing great! Now I want you to take that list and turn the negative beliefs into positive affirmations. Be very positive, not just ho-hum! Be sure that your affirmations are in totally positive language; for example, instead of saying "I'm not stupid!" You would affirm, "I'm intelligent and very capable!" Your positive affirmations might look something like this:

1. I'm an incredible, beautiful human being! I'm a gift to the world!

2. I, (your name), am loveable, and I deserve to be loved!

3. Because I love myself, I'm choosing healthy, loving relationships!

4. In spite of everything I've been through, I'm learning to be a smashing success in life!

5. People love me, because I'm learning to love myself!

6. I'm intelligent, creative, and capable, and I'm finding new and wonderful ways to create success in my life!

7. Everything I plant in life comes up roses!

8. Life is an adventure, and I'm choosing to have a thrilling, exciting ride!

9. My life is full of wonderful surprises! No matter how good my life gets, it can always get better!

10. Happiness is my birthright, and I'm claiming it right now!

3. I'd like you to find some books on positive affirmations that will help you think more of the positive beliefs you may want to program into your unconscious mind. Louise Hay has a wonderful book on using affirmations. Louise is a well-known author and publisher for books about self-esteem and healing. Her book is called *I Can Do It: How to Use Affirmations to Change Your Life*. She also has an audio CD called *101 Power Thoughts* that I would highly recommend!

4.   There are also other books available on affirmations. Go to the library or to a bookstore near you and look around. Sometimes you can just skim through a book and find more positive affirmations that you want to personally program into your mind. Write a list of the affirmations you want to use in your journal.

5.   Now I'd like you to get yourself a blank tape and a simple tape player. With your lists of positive affirmations on front of you, make yourself a tape, using your own voice. Repeat each affirmation twice on the tape, with a space of time after each time you affirm it, so that when you listen to the tape you can repeat the affirmation back to yourself while you are listening. Then go on to the next affirmation till you have them all on your tape.

6.   I want you to think of some times of your day when no one is around and you are doing mundane things, when you can listen to this tape and repeat the affirmations back to yourself. Maybe you could listen to it while you are getting dressed in the morning, or while you're doing the dishes, or maybe even while you're driving to work. What I'd like you to do is play the tape once a day, every day. When you play it back, remember to affirm the new beliefs as you listen to them. Then keep listening to the tape until you really start to believe those new affirmations, and you can see them starting to come true in your life.

7.   I'd suggest you continue listening to this tape every day for a full month to really program those affirmations into your brain. After the first month is over, you may want to make another tape and do the same process using new affirmations that you want to program into your mind. As you keep growing and changing, you'll find new affirmations that are right and appropriate for what you are working on at the moment. Changing your negative beliefs and reprogramming your unconscious mind is a very powerful process, and if you practice it regularly it will undoubtedly change your life!

8. Next, I'd like you to pay attention to your thoughts throughout the day and every time you catch yourself thinking a negative thought, change it to a positive thought. For example, if you wake up in the morning thinking, "Oh, no, I have to get up and go to work and I really don't want to," you could change it to "Hey, it's a brand new day! I'm going to find a way to have some fun today!"

    Make it your goal to change at least three negative thoughts a day to positive ones and then watch and see what happens in your life. I'm pretty sure that you'll be pleasantly surprised! I'd like you to keep track of some of the negative thoughts you changed to positive ones in your journal every day. It will be fun and it will help you see your own progress.

9. Before you go to bed tonight and tomorrow, find your journal and write three successes you had today, three things you feel grateful for, and three desires you have for the future. If you enjoy this process, it's a good one to continue for the next few months. It will help you get into the habit of focusing on the positive in your everyday life.

10. Another book that's very helpful for changing your negative thinking is Martin Seligman's book *Learned Optimism, How to Change Your Mind and Change Your Life*. It's great for getting yourself out of negativity and depression.

11. Now I'd like you to write a few pages about how you feel after changing your negative thoughts and beliefs to positive ones and affirming the positive to yourself regularly.

Good job! You're making great progress! Just keep up the good work! I know you have what it takes to heal. It's just having a clear intention and an on-going persistence. In other words, just don't give up till you make it. I know it can be challenging, but it's so worth it in the end!

Chapter Six

Love Your Body and Love Your Life!

Rachel

Rachel was a beautiful teenage girl who came to me for therapy a few years ago because she was bulimic. She came from a loving family with parents who were still married and who obviously adored her. Her father was somewhat controlling but he doted on Rachel and he would never have hurt her intentionally.

Through therapy we discovered that when Rachel was a small child she overheard her Dad saying negative things about an older sister. Although Rachel was very small at the time, she was hurt by her Dad's negative comments about her sister, whom she loved very dearly. She didn't know how to talk about her feelings so she kept them inside and tried to go on with her life.

As time went on, Rachel kept more and more feelings inside. She was afraid that her Dad would also find negative things to say about her, so she worked very hard to try to please him. She didn't want his negative judgments to ever fall on her. She became obsessed with trying to be perfect in every way, including always trying to look perfect and have a perfect body.

Eventually Rachel needed an outlet for all the feelings she

had stuffed in her unconscious mind, so she became bulimic and started to purge regularly. In therapy, I helped Rachel become conscious and aware of her feelings and learn to express them in healthy ways. I also asked Rachel to write about her feelings in her journal when she had the urge to purge.

Within a few months of writing about her feelings in her journal and working through her deeper feelings in therapy, Rachel was able to resolve the issues with her Dad related to his judgments of her sister. She and her Dad grew closer emotionally and more open in their communication. Before long, Rachel had stopped purging and had healed her emotional backlog. Soon she came to thank me and tell me she wouldn't need my help any longer.

Days 11 and 12

Hello! Welcome back! I'm so happy that you've decided to take this journey with me. Doesn't it feel wonderful to make these changes in your life? I'll bet you're feeling so good that you're wondering what took you so long! Are you smiling right now? I am! This is pretty amazing stuff, isn't it? The things you're doing along the way seem so small by themselves, but when you add them all together, they sure make some dramatic changes in your attitudes, don't they?

So today we're going to talk about loving your body. Hey, wait! Please don't run away, and please don't burn this book! I know loving your body is a challenge for some of you, but this is very important! You can't fully love yourself without loving your body because your body is an important part of you.

We'd better start by getting on the same page. Some of you who already enjoy looking in the mirror may be wondering why it's so difficult for people to love their bodies. Let me explain. If you were verbally, physically or sexually abused, you probably already know the answer. People who experienced abuse often take the bad feelings from the abuse very personally and associate those bad feelings with their perception of their bodies.

For example, a woman who was sexually abused will often turn the disgusting, horrible feelings from the abuse into believing that her body is disgusting and horrible. I know that doesn't make sense logically, but it happens every day. So in the process of healing the effects of her abuse, it's very important that she learns to take back the sweet innocence and natural beauty of her physical body. Trust me, I know that's not an easy task, but I also know you can do it, if you are committed and persistent about making the change.

In the same way, a man who was physically abused could take the mean, hateful feelings from the physical abuse and associate them with his body. So in the process of undoing the damage from the physical abuse, he would also need to learn to love his naturally strong, handsome body.

For you abuse survivors, you may be saying, "Why would I want to love this body? It's given me nothing but grief and pain in my life!" It's true that when you disown your body, and treat it with hate and disgust, it will definitely give you grief and pain. If you want your body to be good to you, you have to be good to your body.

Hospitals and doctor's offices are filled every day with people who have disconnected themselves from their natural, healthy bodies. *When you deny your emotional pain and hate the body that was given to you, you can expect to spend a lot of time and energy focusing on what's wrong with you physically.* To me, that's an extremely boring waste of good energy. But in the same way, if you want to turn the tide and treat your body with love and respect on a daily basis, then in time your body will respond and give you back that love and respect.

Don't panic, I'm not suggesting that we can control our bodies and never have any physical ailments. I'm not trying to play God! I'm just suggesting that if we use those physical ailments as signals from our unconscious mind of what is off track in our mind-body connection and work on the issues emotionally as well as physically, then we can begin to heal the damage that was done by our dysfunctional past.

For twenty years I've kept a copy of a book by Louise Hay called *You Can Heal Your Life* on my desk at my psychotherapy office. Louise Hay's book has an extensive list of physical illnesses and maladies and their emotional and psychological causes. Whenever a client tells me about a physical ache or pain they're experiencing when we're working together, I pull out Louise Hay's book and check for it's emotional or psychological cause. I never cease to be amazed at how accurate Louise's work is, because without fail, whatever my client and I are dealing with emotionally in therapy is the same thing that shows up for that specific physical issue in Louise's list. Often my client and I end up laughing because of how accurate the book is and how uncanny it is that someone out there could know exactly what is going on!

So the bottom line is, there is no escape from your body. You can deal with your issues emotionally or you can deal with them physically, so which would you prefer? *Do you want to hang out in doctor's offices and hospitals for the rest of your life, or do you want to take the 'bull by the horns' and choose to do the work it takes to get healthy emotionally and physically?*

Some of you might enjoy the attention you get from going to doctors and hospitals if you didn't get the love and support you needed from your parents. In therapy, we call that 'secondary gain.' Secondary gain is like having a hidden agenda for being sick, because you don't know how to get your emotional needs met directly.

Don't worry; I have no desire to take away any means you have created to get love and emotional support. Doctors are often kind, loving souls who truly want you to be healthy and happy, and that does feel good when you're hurting emotionally. I'm just suggesting that you might want to consider finding healthier, less expensive way to get love and support.

So let's move on. Another part of loving your body is facing your addictions. Are you ready? Let's be honest! What are you addicted to? Cigarettes? Alcohol? Drugs? Unhealthy foods? What do you suppose those things do to your body? Do you really want to do that to your body if you love it? I know it's never easy to give up addictions. I have great admiration for those of you who decide to do it and actually follow through on your commitment. I know it's a real challenge!

Did you know that your addictions are just another way you have denied and hidden your emotional pain from yourself? When you give up the addiction, guess what comes to the surface? You're right. It's your emotional pain. It's all the feelings you didn't want to deal with! You stuffed them away with the addiction and maybe you even forgot they were there, but here they are, sad to say, and you still get to deal with them.

I know it's a big challenge letting go of addictions. Some of you may need professional help to get through your addictions, but trust me; it's so worth it in the end. Just think of you body like a small child that you love dearly, and then make a commitment to do whatever it takes to treat your body with love and respect. Then go find the help you need to break your addiction. You and everyone around you will benefit when you get healthy. It will be worth everything you put into it!

While we're talking about loving your body, you also may need to face the reality of any self-destructive behavior you are doing that affects your body negatively. Some of you who were severely abused may have developed self-destructive habits to release the emotional pain, like anorexia, bulimia, cutting yourself, picking on your face, or even pulling out your eyelashes.

These self-destructive habits can become very addictive in themselves, because you simply don't know how to release your emotional pain in healthier ways. *If you do any of these behaviors, you will need professional help to get through your deep emotional issues.* Call someone today and set up an appointment.

Remember that you are a special, beautiful spirit and you are simply freeing yourself of negative behaviors you took on long ago to deal with your intense emotional pain. There is definitely a better way to deal with the pain. I know you'll find your way out of the pain with the help of this book and your personal caring psychotherapist.

Before we move on, I want to tell you something exciting that I've learned recently that's related to loving your body. It's one of the most amazing things I've been able to add to my psychotherapy practice in the past few years. You see, I've been doing psychotherapy and emotional healing with people for many years, but a few years ago I became very interested in releasing physical pain as well. I began an intense search to find people who were doing physical healing whom I could learn from. I wanted to find out if spiritual healing was simply a gift that only some people had been given or if normal people like myself could learn skills that would release physical symptoms.

After a few ho-hums and disappointments, I learned of Dr. Kam Yuen who is doing amazing mind-body work. Some of you may remember Dr. Yuen from the TV show *Kung Fu* that was around in the 1980s and 1990s. *Kung-Fu* was based on Dr. Yuen's life and David Carradine played the character of Dr. Yuen in the TV series. The show was a huge hit for many years, but after it completed Dr. Yuen went on to become a chiropractor. He practiced western chiropractic medicine for a time until he realized that it wasn't working as well as the ancient Chinese energetics his ancestors had used in China.

Dr. Yuen went back to China and studied his ancient family heritage, and now he teaches his amazing mind-body technique to thousands of dedicated students. After seeing him the first time, I was determined to learn his process. For the past several years I've been training with Dr. Yuen and practicing his technique daily. You'd be totally amazed at how well it works! It's been a remarkable experience for me, as well as for my clients.

Let me give you an example, okay? Just yesterday I worked with two strong, macho guys in my office. They were completely unrelated to each other, but they both came in with intense physical pain. One of them had not been able to sleep for weeks and the other had been to every doctor and specialist he could find and no one could help him. So here comes the good part! After a normal hour's session with each of them, both of them left my office pain free. Isn't that incredible?

What I've learned in the last few years is that illness and chronic pain are just another way that our emotional pain manifests. For some of us it's easier to feel pain physically than it is to bear the intense, emotional pain from our past. Sometimes the emotional pain is simply too overwhelming and we unconsciously turn it into physical pain.

It's very exciting to watch the responses in my clients when we do the Yuen Method Wellness technique and their physical pain often just disappears right on the spot. They are generally dumbfounded in disbelief! After all, our entire belief system is based on our total helplessness to affect or overcome our physical pains.

We have, as a culture, believed for centuries that health is a gift that we are either fortunate enough to receive, or we're not. Few of us have realized that we play a part in choosing our health or our lack of it. Thinking of chronic pain and physical health in this way is a new paradigm for the western world and it takes time to adjust to those new ways of thinking.

So, let's talk about what you can do right now to start loving your body. I know you've got a lot to think about today with everything we've been discussing. I also know that you probably don't have the tools available to you today to release all your body aches and pains, but I'm not letting you off the hook, because I know that you can still start loving your body today!

The first, most obvious way to love our body on a daily basis is to pay attention to it. Notice what your body feels and what it needs and try to give your body what it needs whenever you can. For example, if you regularly breathe short shallow breaths, your body may need some deep cleansing, releasing breaths.

If you've been sitting around for a long time, your body may need to get outside, and move around and breathe some fresh air. Or if you've been working hard for days on end, your body may need a break. Maybe it's time for some rest and relaxation. Don't expect your body to be like a machine that never stops. Instead treat it like a special, very important part of you that you love and respect.

You can probably guess two of the next important parts of loving your body. Most people hear them everyday these days. They are, of course, eating healthy and exercising regularly! I'm not going to go into great depth about how to eat healthy or how to exercise. There are lots of books already written about that by people much more knowledgeable than me. I'll just cover a few of the basics and then you can find some books at your library or bookstore that go more in depth.

Let's do exercising first, because that's a little easier. There are hundreds of ways to get exercise, from walking or jogging, to working out in the gym, or doing yogi, or playing tennis or dancing. It really doesn't matter which one you choose. Maybe if you listen to your body, it will tell which one it prefers.

The important thing is to do something, and do it regularly. Your body needs to move regularly if you want it to be healthy and happy. Moving regularly means exercising for 30 minutes at least three times a week. I personally prefer exercise that gets you out in nature, because not only do you move your body, but you also get to experience the beauty of nature and feel close to God while you're doing it.

Eating healthy foods might be a more difficult habit to change for some of you. None of us eats perfectly these days, especially with all the goodies that are available to us at a minute's notice. I'm not asking for perfection. I simply would like to see you start making small changes towards eating healthier, as a way to show your body how much you love it and want it to be healthy and happy.

Are you wondering what changes you could make? You could start with eating less fast food, and more fresh fruits and vegetables. Then, when your body adjusts to that, you could also eliminate white flour and white sugar in your diet. You may be saying, "Wait a minute! What does that leave for me to eat?" It leaves fruits, vegetables, whole grain carbohydrates and lean meats or proteins. Believe it or not, there are actually many yummy foods in that group.

You see, your body needs food that is alive and growing, not food that is packaged and sitting on the shelf for years on end. If you love your precious son or daughter, or even your favorite dog or cat, wouldn't you want to give them healthy nutritious food that will give them healthy, happy bodies that last for a lifetime? Then why wouldn't you do the same for yourself, if you love your own body?

I know, that's the problem, isn't it? Maybe you don't really love your body. Do you think giving yourself a donut when you're feeling sad or lonely is love? That's not love; it's addiction. Love is doing what's right and good for your body that will pay off over the long haul. It's not just a quick fix for today.

I can see we need to do some work on loving your body, so here's the most important part of today's lesson. I saved the best for last because I knew it might be scary for you. Here's the secret for today. *If you want to really learn to love your body, it's important to practice standing in front of the mirror in the nude every day and saying "I love you just the way you are!"*

Okay, take a big, deep breath. I'm serious! Let me say it one more time. If you want to really learn to love your body, practice standing in front of your mirror in the nude and saying "I love you" to your body every day. It's very powerful! I once heard a story of a woman who lost a hundred pounds by making only that one change in her life.

I'm sure you are very anxious to get started with your homework today, so let's go for it, okay? I've got some great homework for you. You'll probably hate it and love it, but in the end you'll be grateful, because your body will be so happy to reconnect with you and be a healthy part of your life. Relax! Remember it's never as bad as you think it will be.

Homework Assignment: Chapter Six

1. What negative things happened to your body when you were a child that may have caused you to disconnect and hate your body? Write a few paragraphs about that, and then also write about how you could love and accept your body more today.

2. What are you addicted to? Are you addicted to cigarettes, alcohol, drugs or unhealthy foods? Write a paragraph about what you could do in the next few months to let go of those addictions.

3. Are you doing any self-destructive behaviors? Write a few paragraphs about the behaviors you know you need to release. If you are doing self-destructive behaviors, you will definitely need to get professional help. Look in the yellow pages and find someone to call today for help in releasing those behaviors.

4. Pay attention to your body and ask it what it feels and needs at least ten times today and tomorrow. One way to do that is to set your watch alarm to go off every hour on the hour. When the alarm goes off, just take some big deep breaths and check in with your body. Ask it what it feels and what it needs and then try to give it love and attention whenever you can. If your body tells you it wants rest and

relaxation, have some fun thinking about what you could do to make your body happy! Then don't forget to do it!

5. Now, think of a physical activity you could do today that gets you up and moving. What do you most enjoy? Do you like to walk, or dance, or do yogi? It doesn't matter which one you pick, but do something for at least 30 minutes 3 times this week. When you finish exercising each day, I'd like you to write about how you felt while you exercised, okay?

6. Please keep a journal today and tomorrow about every thing you eat. Whenever possible, substitute healthy, life-giving foods for unhealthy ones, and write about how you feel doing that. Make it your goal to make small changes in your diet over time until you get it to the point where you can see the changes in your body and you feel good about it.

7. When you get up in the morning or after your shower, stand in front of your mirror in the nude and practice saying the words "_____, I love you just the way you are!" Say it at least ten times every day this week, and then write about how that felt for you.

8. A few books I'd recommend on healing your body are:
    Adam, *DreamHealer 2, Guide to Self-Empowerment*
    Louise Hay, *You Can Heal Your Life*
    John E. Sarno, MD, *The Mind-Body Prescription*
    Candace Pert, *Molecules of Emotion; The Science Behind Mind-Body Medicine*
    Caroline Myss, *Why People Don't Heal and How They Can*
    Eleanor Limmer, *Balance, Beyond Illness to Health and Wholeness*
    Brandon Bays, *The Journey, A Road Map to the Soul*
    Dr. Kam Yuen, *Instant Pain Elimination; How to stop the pain you feel in 2 minutes or less.*

9. If you're interested in learning more about Dr. Kam Yuen and his Yuen Method Wellness technique, you can go to his website at www.Yuenmethod.com and read more about his work. You can also read some testimonials of clients I've worked with on my website at www.kari-joys.com.

10. Write a few pages in your journal about how you feel after doing today's homework.

Wow! I'm so proud of you! Doesn't it feel good to really love your body and treat it with love and respect ever day? You've made some very important changes here, and you're going to be so glad you did! Keep up the good work!

Chapter Seven

Forgive the Past and Take Back Your Spiritual Power!

Lisa

Lisa was the third of four children in a hard working, pioneer type family in Montana. Her mother was an old-fashioned lady with a big heart, known by many as a great cook and gardener. Her father was a self-made businessman, who had grown up with very little and made a good life for himself and his family. Both parents were respected and admired in the community where everyone knew everyone else.

What people didn't know was that Lisa's father was sexually abusing her from a very young age. He also sexually abused Lisa's cousins and a close friend of hers. When Lisa was fourteen, the abuse suddenly stopped. She never knew why until she found out many years later that her father had started sexually abusing her younger sister at that time.

As a teenager, Lisa became very rebellious. She created a wild reputation for herself with drinking and doing drugs. She buried the memories of abuse as deep as she could, and she became very good at faking normalcy, but there was not a day that passed when she didn't think of what had happened.

Lisa surprised everyone by going to college and getting a degree in special education. She taught special education for a few years and then she met her husband. Her husband was the only person who ever knew Lisa's secret through all those years.

Lisa became a stay at home Mom with a steady husband and a beautiful son, but the fake self that had served her so well through the years was beginning to crack. She had horrible depressing memories that would run in her mind, keeping her from enjoying life. She had no self-esteem and no self-respect. She felt lost and hopeless, like her spirit was broken.

The damn finally broke when Lisa's young niece who had been educated about "good touch, bad touch" finally broke the silence. She told Lisa's sister what Grandpa had done to her and Grandpa's secret life began to unravel. The family confronted him and charges were pressed. It was the talk of the town. Lisa and her family felt incredibly humiliated and ashamed. She said it was like being victimized all over again.

The good thing was that it forced Lisa to deal with the reality of her life. A dear friend of hers referred her to me for therapy, and Lisa began her emotional healing journey. She says the love and understanding she felt gave her the courage to work through the emotional pain. She cried buckets of tears and gradually began to put together the fractured parts of herself.

Lisa was very glad she had a chance to work through her feelings before her father passed away. She was able to confront him, question him, and express her intense anger for what he had done. The most confusing thing to her was how someone who loved her could hurt her so badly. Her father could never answer that question. She says she'll never know.

When her father died, Lisa went to the funeral home alone to say good-bye. She cried tears that fell on the hands that had hurt her so badly, but she knew now he could never hurt anyone again. She wondered where his spirit would go, because she thought even Saint Peter would have a quandary with this situation. She asked her father to give her an unmistakable sign that he was okay and that he had made it to the other side.

Friends and neighbors were very kind at her father's funeral. At the burial site, just at the moment the minister was saying his last few words and the casket was being lowered into the ground, a huge flock of geese flew right over the top of the ceremony. The geese were so noisy that they couldn't even hear the minister. Lisa knew at that moment that this was her sign.

Finally Lisa's pain was complete and she was able to forgive her dad and let go. She says she'll carry the scars of sexual abuse throughout her life, but she knows in many ways her difficult childhood has made her a stronger, more compassionate person. The good news is that today Lisa actually loves herself!

Days 13 and 14

Hello again! How are you doing today? Are you feeling overwhelmed? Don't worry! Resolving the past and choosing lightheartedness is a monumental undertaking. It's not a job for the 'faint of heart.' But on the other hand, remember that God never gives you more than you can handle. You can do anything you set your mind to do.

Just don't give up! If it seems overwhelming, or if you have a lot of hurt, or sad, or angry feelings going on today, I'd suggest that you go back to Chapter Three before you continue and work through those old feelings. When the old feelings are cleared out, and you're back to feeling peaceful inside, it becomes so much easier to take in this new information and move forward.

So today we're going to talk about forgiveness. Forgiveness is a difficult topic for many people who grew up in dysfunctional families. I just want you to know that it was challenging for me too. What I'm sharing with you is the result of many years of working not only with my own healing, but also with thousands of clients who passed through my doors to heal and resolve their dysfunctional family issues.

First of all, I want to say very clearly that forgiveness doesn't mean condoning a wrong that someone did to you. If you were abused or neglected as a child, it's never going to be okay that someone did that to you. Simply by existing on this planet, you are "a child of the Universe no less than the trees and the stars" according to the ancient Desiderata. So you definitely deserved better than abuse and neglect, even if it was emotional abuse and neglect.

Every child who is born on this earth deserves to be loved, and every child deserves to be protected every day of his or her life. That definitely includes you! Forgiveness never means that we are making it okay that you were abused or mistreated in any way.

I grew up in a traditional church where we were taught to 'forgive and forget' anything and everything anyone did to hurt us. To me, as a child, that translated into thinking that forgiveness meant that it was okay for people to abuse me and that I should smile and be happy with whatever treatment I got.

I thought forgiveness was for the benefit of the abuser. I thought it was giving them a clean slate so they could repeat their behavior over and over again and never be held responsible. It seemed like the abuser was getting off the hook and that if I agreed to forgive, I was agreeing to condone his or her total lack of responsibility for the hurt or pain that he or she was causing others.

What I learned from years of therapy was that forgiveness is actually for the benefit of the person who was wounded, not the abuser. I also learned that even if I forgave someone it didn't mean I had to trust him or her again if they were not trustworthy. It didn't mean that I ever had to be close friends with them if they hadn't taken responsibility for their actions and made sincere amends. But I learned that when I held on to the hurt and pain from my past and lived my life focused on that hurt and pain, it tied up my emotional energy so much that I had no energy left to create the life I wanted to create.

So you see, choosing to forgive and release the past just frees you up to use your energy for positive things in your life. Sometimes you have to forgive someone over and over in the process of your healing, because there's so much emotional damage they caused in your life that you can't forgive it all in one day. But if you continue to forgive again and again whenever it comes up, eventually there is nothing left to forgive. When that happens, then you are free to become the person you really want to be in the world.

Sometimes we find it difficult to forgive someone because we are still trying to get the love we need from the person who hurt us. In our magical thinking, we believe that holding on to the pain until they are genuinely sorry will somehow help us get the love we need. If you're still doing that, you may as well give it up! It simply doesn't work. There are some people who simply don't know how to love. You can hold out for a lifetime, but they will never change. You know the old saying; "You can't get blood out of a turnip!"

The good news is that when we finally forgive the people who hurt us and let go of the past, there are always other people waiting who want to love us. *Love is everywhere, when we open our hearts.* You can honestly receive love from a stranger you meet for the first time on the street when your heart is open. But holding a grudge and trying to force someone to love you the way you think they should is a thankless, useless occupation. It's a horrible waste of your valuable time and energy. Give it up, forgive, let go, and open your heart to find the people who really want and are able to love you.

Sometimes it helps to create a ritual of some kind to really let go. If that feels good to you, you can create your own ritual that's perfect for you personally. For example, you could take everything you have that reminds you of the person who hurt you and go out in the woods and do your own private ritual of forgiving and letting go, and then bury or burn everything you've brought with you. Or, if you prefer, you could do a meditation where you imagine doing the ritual. A ritual of forgiving and letting go sometimes helps our unconscious mind really understand at a gut level that we're serious about moving forward in our lives. Moving forward is what really matters..

While we're on the topic of forgiveness, it's also very important that you forgive yourself. Growing up in a dysfunctional family means you usually didn't get the guidance and support you needed to be the person you wanted to be, so there are probably things about yourself that you are not very happy about. You undoubtedly made some mistakes in your life, but remember that everybody makes mistakes, and mistakes can be very valuable experiences when we learn from them. Maybe you think your mistakes are unforgivable, and that nobody can ever love you after what you've done, but nothing is unforgivable to God. Remember that God loves you unconditionally! God always sees you through the eyes of compassion.

If you have committed crimes in your life, you may have to pay the worldly consequences for what you've done, but to God, you are forgiven even before you ask. It may also be important to go to the people you have hurt in your life and ask them for forgiveness, or make sincere amends in some way for the damage you have done. That's part of being a responsible, caring, healthy adult. But when you have sincerely made amends, and learned what not to do next time the same situation arises, then you need to forgive yourself and give yourself a clean slate to go forward in life. It's so freeing to let go of all that old baggage. You're going to feel so much better when it's finally gone!

Sometimes we have to forgive God before we can really move forward in our lives. Many of us were taught as children that God was supposed to be there for us, and meet our needs, and protect us from harm. When that didn't happen the way we thought it should, we may have given up on God completely. Sometimes we have even stopped trusting that there is a Higher Power in the world that wants us to be happy.

When you stop believing in a Higher Power, you will often start believing in your fear. Like we discussed yesterday, when you believe in your fear, you always prepare yourself for the worst that could possibly happen and expect the worst. Living that way sets you up for more negative, painful things to happen in your life, because your consciousness is vibrating at the level of pain and negativity.

Remember that God always says, "Yes!" to you. If you believe in your fear, you will get more negative experiences. If you believe in a Higher Power, however, and you put your energy into expecting good to come to you, your positive vibration will draw that good to you.

We may have different beliefs about who God is, and that's totally okay. I don't need for you to agree with my belief system. But when you do your homework today, I'd like you to simply think of God as a Higher Power that wants good for you and wants you to be happy. This Higher Power may not have saved you from the pain in your life, but it definitely gave you the strength to survive. God doesn't take away people's choices, even when those choices are abusive of others, but he does give survivors the spiritual strength to overcome the pain.

Now that you are an adult and you are no longer dependent on people who can hurt you or abuse you, you can call on God or your Higher Power at any time and actually see the results that happen in your life. When you call on your Higher Power in your mind, you are actually praying. Prayer is just talking to God in your heart about whatever concerns you and asking for help and guidance to bring about a positive resolution to the problem.

Before we complete today, there's one more thing I'd really like you to understand. It's very difficult to create a healthy life and learn to live lightheartedly when you cannot call on God or your Higher Power to help you accomplish it. By ourselves, we are just little human beings trying to survive in a big scary world. But when we forgive God, and join forces with our Higher Power, suddenly we have a tremendous spiritual power available to us. God can do anything! When we call on God for help, we, too, can accomplish amazing things that we never would have dreamed possible before.

So let's get to work. We've got a lot to do today! This is some of the most powerful work you'll ever do for yourself!

Homework Assignment: Chapter Seven

1. Make a list of the people who are still difficult for you to forgive. Be sure to think carefully of everyone that is important to you who still brings up negative feelings for you in any way when you think of them, or when you have contact with them.

2. In your journal, start with the people who are difficult to forgive today in your present life, and then go to your parents or your early caregivers. Then taking them one at a time, I want you to write a journal letter to each one, starting with "Dear_____".
    I'd like you to include six things in each letter.
    a.What they did that hurt you.

b.What you needed, or what you still need from them, that you never got.

c. What you learned from having them in your life.

d. Your intention to forgive them, to let go, and to release the past.

e. Imagine a ritual where you carry out the letting go process, and tell them about it.

f. Sincerely wish them well in their life, because that's where true forgiveness ends. You're letting go and letting God be in charge of any consequences they may have for what they did that hurt you.

Do not send these letters unless you feel certain that what you have written would benefit your relationship and would cause no harm! Keep them for yourself, or burn them to let go of the emotional energy. What we're doing here is for your benefit more than for anyone else. When the energy shifts between you and that person as a result of the forgiveness you are doing here, your relationship with them will change naturally.

3.   If it's difficult for you to forgive and let go, write about your resistance, or the part of you that doesn't want to forgive. What does this part of you want to accomplish by hanging on to your anger or hurt? What is your payoff for holding on to the past? Do you think holding on to the hurt will make someone finally love you the way you need to be loved? Do you want to punish the person who hurt you? Do you need to file legal charges against them? If you need to file charges, then do it, but also continue working towards forgiveness of that person even while you are holding them legally responsible for their behavior.

4.   If it's still difficult to forgive, write a paragraph about who you believe is being hurt more by you not forgiving. Is it the person you are angry with, or it is you? Research has shown that people who hold on to their anger long-term are more likely to get debilitating illnesses. Do you really want to hurt yourself by holding on to the past?

5. The next person you need to forgive is yourself. I'd like for you to make a list of the things you have done in your life that have hurt other people. If you haven't already apologized and asked their forgiveness, then it's time to do that now.

    Start with writing a letter to each person you have hurt, apologizing sincerely and asking their forgiveness, and asking them what you could do to make amends for any damage you have done in their life. *You may want to actually send these letters, if you haven't already asked forgiveness of these people, unless asking forgiveness and making amends to them now would hurt them in some way.*

6. When that's complete, write a letter to yourself. List the things you feel you need forgiveness for and write your intention to forgive and let go of the past. When you have done that, write a sincere prayer to God asking for divine help in forgiving yourself for the past and starting fresh today to live a healthier, happier life.

7. Now I'd like you to write a forgiveness letter to God or your Higher Power. I want you to think of all the times you thought that God had let you down in your life. Write a letter to God including these five steps:
    a. When and how you thought God let you down in your life.
    b. What you needed from God that you didn't get.
    c. What you understand about God today that you didn't understand in the past.
    d. Your intention to forgive God, and give your Higher Power another chance in your life.
    e. A sincere prayer to ask God to help you let go of the hurt and pain of the past and move forward into a new and better life.

8. There are a couple of books about forgiveness I'd recommend. One is Gerald G. Jampolsky's *Love is letting Go Of Fear*. It's an old standard that has helped people choose love and forgiveness in their lives for many years. If you're feeling especially courageous today, there's also a book called *Radical Forgiveness* that I would highly rec-

ommend. You may not agree with everything it says, but it definitely has substantial food for thought. The author, Colin Tipping, believes that *Radical Forgiveness* could change the world we live in.

9.   Write a few pages about how you feel today after writing your forgiveness letters. Remember that hot-pen technique; just write, write, write! Don't censor anything.

If today's homework takes a week instead of a couple of days, it's well worth your time! I'd suggest that you do not move forward with your 33-day journey until you have completed this process.

Wow, that was a big job, wasn't it? I sincerely want to congratulate you today for having the courage to face the people who hurt you the most and being willing to forgive them and let go of the pain. Good work! I never said this would be easy, but I know for sure that it will be worth your work and time! Hang in there! Before long, you'll see what I mean.

Chapter Eight

Identify with the Strength of Your Spirit, Not Your History!

Jessica

Jessica was born when her mother was only sixteen years old. Her parent's divorced when she was five and she never saw her father again. A neighbor man bribed Jessica to come into his house during that same year and sexually abused her.

Jessica's mother began using drugs and alcohol after the divorce and became very promiscuous. After a series of boyfriends, she settled with a verbally and physically abusive man and had two more children. Jessica remembers her mother and her new stepfather screaming and fighting regularly during that period of her young life. When she was only six and seven years old, Jessica was often left alone to care for her brothers.

When Jessica was eight, she begged her Grandma to let her come live with her. Grandma reluctantly took Jessica in but often reminded her what a burden she was and gave Jessica only the minimal support she needed to survive. Jessica's aunts who lived nearby were not supportive either and they often encouraged Grandma to give Jessica over to the state. They also told Jessica regularly that she would undoubtedly turn out just like her mother.

Jessica's Grandma made it very clear to Jessica that she would have to move out when she turned eighteen. Jessica was afraid to live on her own, so when a boy she was dating joined the Air Force and asked her to marry him and move to Japan, she quickly agreed.

Jessica's new husband was also from a very dysfunctional family. Jessica knew that they had married too young. There were many power struggles in their marriage. Jessica says she and her new husband *needed* each other much more than they actually *loved* each other. After four years of living in Japan, Jessica and her husband moved back to the States and gave birth to a son.

Postpartum depression set in for Jessica after her son was born. The responsibility of raising a child after her own dysfunctional childhood was just too much for her to manage. She says she felt like she had hit a brick wall and didn't know where to turn. A friend of hers suggested counseling and referred her to me.

The journey to emotional health for Jessica was enlightening and refreshing. Jessica says it was a joy to have someone genuinely listen and care. No one had ever validated her strengths before or affirmed her natural talents. Jessica's depression lifted as she began to trust herself and pay attention to her own feelings.

As Jessica continued her emotional healing journey, she began to connect back to some powerful feelings she had as young child. At four and five years old, Jessica had intense feelings of being a spirit who had come into a physical body with an important purpose to fulfill.

She remembers writing a poem when she was about ten years old that described a memory she had that took place before her birth. Jessica saw herself as an angel flying around the world looking down and seeing all the problems in the world and wanting to help the world heal. Reconnecting to those childhood memories helped Jessica regain a sense of her true self and to her spiritual purpose in the world.

At the age of twenty-six, Jessica's life is still not perfect, but she says she feels much stronger now. After growing up in the dysfunctional way she did, Jessica is very dedicated to raising her young son in a healthy, loving environment. She is also currently finishing a degree in massage therapy. Jessica plans to support herself and her son with her massage practice while she pursues her loftier dreams and goals.

In the long term, Jessica wants to delve into research on what makes the world work. Societies and cultures fascinate her, as well as what makes cultures form and grow. Jessica says she has a dream to research the mind-body-spirit connection and by doing that to completely revolutionize western medicine. Identifying with her true spirit and believing in her dreams will undoubtedly prove to be a powerful motivation and impetus in Jessica's life!

Days 15 and 16

So how are you doing today? Are you feeling emotionally drained from your forgiveness letters yesterday? Are you physically exhausted? Emotional work can be very draining. Trust me, I know that. I work with it every day! Well, don't worry. You can relax, because this lesson will be easier. I knew you needed a lighter assignment after all that hard work. So we're going to do some fun things today.

We talk a lot about the difficulty and pain that comes from growing up in a dysfunctional family, but it's also very interesting to turn the tables and think about the good that comes from growing up that way. Are you ready to give it a try? I'd like you to try focusing for a moment on what you learned from growing up in your family of origin. What positive qualities do you now have that came out of overcoming the pain of your childhood? What strengths have you found within yourself to survive? Have those strengths ever benefited your life in any way? Did growing up the way you did make you more compassionate of others? Sometimes our greatest woundedness becomes our greatest strength!

I know for myself that I wouldn't be the person I am today if I had not been abused as a child. You might say that knowing that doesn't condone abusing an innocent child. I totally agree! On a personal level, no one had the right to abuse me or treat me unkindly as a child. I was innocent and pure-hearted and, like you and many others who were abused, all I ever wanted was to be loved and accepted.

But spiritually, I still have to say that I'd never be the person I am today as an adult if I had not experienced the pain of abuse. I wouldn't be as caring and compassionate of others. I wouldn't be as strong as a person, and as deep in my understanding of life and the people on this planet. I wouldn't be able to help other people heal from dysfunctional family issues in the same way, because I wouldn't know how they feel. So even though I will always believe that child abuse is very wrong and that all children deserve to be loved and protected, another part of me suspects that maybe God had some plan in allowing the abuse to happen in my life. I think it's really true that our greatest strength often comes from our greatest woundedness!

So I'd like you to play a game with me for a moment. I'd like you to consider the possibility that maybe your family of origin was actually a part of the Divine plan for your life in some way. Have you ever thought of that? What if, before you were born, when you were still a little spirit looking down from the clouds, you and God and your angel guides discussed what you wanted to accomplish in this lifetime? What if you thought of the spiritual qualities you would need to fulfill your spiritual purpose, and then you looked around at all the possible families you could be born into, and you chose the one that would best help you develop those qualities?

I know it's very hard to consider that possibility when you're still hurting from the pain of your life. That's why I waited to suggest these ideas until you had a chance to release your feelings and do your forgiveness letters. If what we're discussing today brings up more feelings, you can always go back to the homework in Chapter Three and work though those feelings again before you start today's homework. If this thirty-three day journey takes ninety days for you, it's still well worth your time!

It's probably better for you to wait to do this homework until you're in a peaceful state of mind. So if you're feeling peaceful today and if you have the emotional energy to face a new way of looking at the world, I'm just asking that you give these ideas a little time and thought. I think you'll find it to be very freeing.

So here's the secret for today; if you want to learn how to be authentically light-hearted, it's very important that you learn to identify with the strength of your spirit rather than with your painful history. Identifying yourself with the pain of your history keeps you stuck in a rut that you never get out of, like trying to climb out of that pickle jar we were discussing earlier. But identifying with the strength of your spirit gives you a whole new approach to life. The opportunities you have before you now are limitless!

Just think about it for a moment! If, when you were just a little, innocent child, with no help, and no support, and no one to count on, you still managed to survive the pain of your dysfunctional family and grow up to be a reasonably healthy adult, what does that say about what you might be able to accomplish today if you set your mind to it? Maybe it's not too late to go after those goals you have always wanted to accomplish. Maybe you could find a way to overcome the challenges of your life and fulfill your lifelong dreams. What an exciting thought!

I can hardly wait to get to the homework today, can you? I love seeing people get better! That's what makes my work so much fun! You see, my dear, you are on the road to success! There's nowhere to go from here but up. You and I are going to have so much fun! Please, go get your notebook. We've got work to do!

Homework Assignment: Chapter Eight

1. I want you to write a few paragraphs in your journal about why you and God and your angel guides may have chosen this particular family of origin for you when you were looking down from the clouds trying to decide where you wanted to be born. What do you imagine could be the spiritual purpose you may have wanted to fulfill in your life?

2. What qualities do you think you were you trying to develop by choosing this particular family? How did this crazy, dysfunctional family help you develop the qualities and strengths you needed to become the person you wanted to be?

3. Now, I want to ask you a very important question. Brace yourself! Here it is! Right now, today, are you ready to stop being a victim and start identifying yourself with the strength of your spirit? Please give me a straight answer! If your answer is yes, then I want you to write your intention in your journal very clearly, something like this:

    "From this day forward, I, (your name), intend to focus on the strength of my spirit, rather than on the pain of what happened to me in my life. From this point on, I will express the feelings of what happened in the past only long enough to release the emotional pain. Starting today, it is my sincere intention to fully realize the beauty and the strength of the person I was meant to be on the earth and fulfill my spiritual purpose!" Then sign your name and date it. This is a contract you are making with yourself. It is extremely powerful to your unconscious mind to put it down on paper and sign it.

4. Now that you know that you're a courageous survivor who overcame great difficulty in your life to become who you are, what other challenges are you ready to face in your life? What would you like to accomplish in your life that you never thought was possible before? Write a paragraph or two about this and have some fun with this question! Let that playful child in you come out and play with these ideas!

5. There's a book you may want to read if you're particularly interested in this chapter, called *Legacy of the Heart, The Spiritual Advantage of a Painful Childhood,* by Wayne Muller.

6. Write a few pages about how you are feeling after doing today's homework.

Great Job! You're doing great! I knew you could do it! I hope you have a fun day today and tomorrow, just thinking of yourself as a survivor. If you were strong enough to overcome all that pain and trauma in your life, you had to be very courageous and determined! So, watch out world! Your life is changing dramatically even as we speak!

Chapter Nine

Own Your Personal Power and Learn to Set Boundaries!

Kari

I was born the youngest of ten children in a religious family. My mother was a wonderful, kind-hearted woman who truly lived her spirituality but my father was often difficult and controlling. I was raised with the old 'spare the rod and spoil the child' belief system which today would be called verbal and physical abuse.

I was a timid child who wanted love very badly. Our church taught that you should break a child's will at a young age to teach them to obey. They also taught that you should never give a child too much praise or they would become conceited. My longing for pure, unconditional love got lost in the shuffle of too many children in our family and too many old, religious belief systems.

I was also sexually abused and, like many other children, I felt guilty and blamed myself. The church taught that if a man was attracted to a girl, the girl had obviously done something wrong to invite it. There was no way to develop self-esteem in that environment, so I grew up confused, depressed and lonely. No one thought of getting help for me. It simply wasn't done in those days. I escaped into romance novels from the third grade through high school and before I graduated I had read all the romance novels in the entire library in our small town.

As a young adult I acted out my longing for love by becoming addicted to romantic relationships. I went from one partner to the next, always trying to find that illusive, romantic love I had read about in my romance novels. Nothing authentic ever hit the empty spot inside me that needed love so desperately, because I really didn't know what I was looking for.

I was very lucky to get into group therapy at just twenty-two years old. I soon discovered that emotional healing was something that could really make a difference. I worked very hard to heal myself and in the process, I also became fascinated with helping others heal. Only a year later, I was fortunate to be given the opportunity to become a group therapist.

After working as a group therapist for two years, I took time off work to get married, have children and be a stay-at-home Mom. Because I knew the importance of early childhood care and nurturing, I was very determined to be the world's first perfect mother, but of course I wasn't able to achieve that perfection. I wanted more than anything in the world to give my daughters a strong sense of themselves and to have them grow up feeling the unconditional love I had so longed for as a child.

I went back to work as a psychotherapist when my daughters were quite young. I soon became a single parent with all the responsibility of raising my girls and taking care of them financially. It was a tremendous challenge to me! I never wanted my children to feel abused or controlled like I did as a child, so I often went to the other extreme of being too permissive.

Because I raised them to be strong and confident, my daughters were often more confident than I was. Raising them as a single parent became like a home-study course in assertiveness training for me. They had no problem knowing who they were or knowing they were loved, but I was the one who had grow to become a healthy parent. I had to learn how to set clear boundaries with my daughters which wasn't an easy task for me.

Boundaries were also an issue for me in other relationships. I was so programmed as a child to accept whatever I was
given and to tolerate any kind of treatment, that standing my
ground and speaking my truth was often terrifying. Like many
other codependents, it was always easier for me to give in and
tolerate abuse than it was to risk abandonment.

Doing my own emotional healing helped me finally learn
that by setting clear boundaries, everyone was happier, including me. Today people generally experience me as kind, calm
and assertive. My clients laugh when I tell them I used to be
wimpy. I know they have no idea how hard I worked to become
a strong, assertive, compassionate person.

Days 17 and 18

So hello! How are you? Here we are again! You've made it through
two weeks already. Good for you! I'm so proud of you for making the
effort. I'll bet you never thought that getting healthy and learning to
have fun could be so much work! So what is it that you think we psychotherapists do all the time, huh? Do you think we meditate on our
navels and twiddle our thumbs? Relax! I'm just teasing you! Hey, look at
that! We're already becoming more lighthearted. When you can laugh at
yourself, you're well on your way to success!

So today we're going to talk about what love is and what it isn't.
Those of us who grew up in dysfunctional families often have a distorted
view of what love means. Too often, we let people use and abuse us in the
name of love because we think that's what we have to do in order to
have love in our lives. Remember the song "Any kind of love is better than
no love at all?" Well, let me be the first to tell you; that's not healthy thinking! People will use and abuse you as long as you let them, but that's not
love; it's abuse!

Having true, unconditional love means that you listen from your
heart when your loved one shares their joy or their pain. It means that you
put yourself in your loved one's shoes and try to have compassion and
understanding for his or her feelings. True, unconditional love practices

the golden rule of treating others the way you want to be treated. It considers the other person's feelings when you make decisions that affect them. True, unconditional love means you share mutually in joint responsibilities and that you work together towards common goals.

When people truly love you, they treat you the way they want to be treated. They think of your best interests as well as their own. They don't take advantage of you in every way they can and then make excuses for why they hurt you, or why they just can't possibly be there for you when you need something from them. That's not love; it's emotional abuse!

When you allow others to use you, take advantage of you, control you, or to be dishonest or disrespectful to you or to the people that you love, you're not doing it because you love them; you're doing it because you're afraid of being alone or abandoned. You probably tell yourself that this is what you have to tolerate in order to have love in your life, because that's what you learned as a child.

So where did those distorted ideas about love come from? Where else? They came from our dysfunctional families! If you were abused, controlled, disrespected, put down or taken advantage of as a child, that's what you learned to expect in the name of love. You learned to tolerate and survive, because that's the only choice you had when you were small and dependent on the adults who were raising you.

Whatever treatment we experience from our caregivers at an early age defines what we believe is 'love.' If we experience kindness, generosity, and support, we think love is kindness, generosity and support, and we are appalled when others treat us any other way. If, however, we experience disrespect, or verbal, physical, or sexual abuse, we come to believe that disrespect and abuse are love.

Some of you may have read the book *Women Who Love Too Much* by Robin Norwood that was popular back in the 1980s and 1990s. It was a book about women who went from one bad relationship to the next, letting men use and abuse them in the name of love. The women in Robin Norwood's stories obviously had learned early in their lives that love was abuse. No matter how painful their last relationship had been, each time they looked for a new relationship, they looked for what they unconsciously recognized as love. *The sad news is that many women and men are still allowing others to use and abuse them.* Too often, still today, we don't differentiate between emotional abuse and true, unconditional love. Often it's because we don't know how to set clear boundaries in our relationships.

If you're new to personal growth, it's possible that you have never understood the concept of personal boundaries. Most dysfunctional families didn't teach children how to set boundaries for themselves. Often what we learned from our dysfunctional families was that we simply had to tolerate dysfunction and abuse to survive.

Boundaries are clear limits we set with people we love about how we want to be treated or not treated. An example of setting a boundary would be to say "I love you dearly, but I absolutely will not tolerate dishonesty in our relationship. If you lie to me again, you won't have me in your life because I don't want to live that way!" You could set the same boundary with not being willing to tolerate verbal, physical, or sexual abuse or with anything else that feels crucially important to you.

If you grew up in a dysfunctional family, you may not know what boundaries are appropriate to set for yourself. A rule of thumb is to pay attention to your anger, because your anger is often a signal to you that shows you where you need to set clear boundaries. If you find yourself feeling angry with someone in your life on a regular basis, you could ask yourself "What is the boundary I need to set with him or her that will make me feel more comfortable?"

For example, if someone you love puts you down or regularly makes jokes at your expense, you may find yourself feeling very angry and hostile towards him or her. Rather than getting revenge and attacking back, you may need to set a boundary about how you want to be treated in the future. You could say "I don't feel comfortable with your put-downs and your inappropriate jokes at my expense. I don't think it's funny, and I will not tolerate it in the future. If you want to have me in your life, you will have to find a way to treat me with love and respect!"

If you've let people mistreat you in the past, setting boundaries like this may be terrifying to you. You may have to practice over time and work up your courage slowly till you can be completely and totally clear with the people you love.

A good way to practice setting boundaries is to stand in front of your mirror and practice a hundred ways to say "No!" Put your hand over your belly button and practice saying "No!" emphatically from your gut. For example, you could say "No, I don't want to!" or "No, I'm not interested!" or "No, I don't have time!" or "No, that's not how I see it!" or you could say "What part of 'no' don't you understand?"

Be sure you are saying "No!" with a clear, strong emphasis, like you really mean it. If you say it in a wimpy way, you give a double message. The person who is abusing you still gets the underlying message that they can convince you to do what they want, despite your wimpy words of displeasure. You'll need to practice speaking up daily and saying what you mean as clearly, concisely, and emphatically as you possibly can. Eventually, if you continue practicing this over time, you will see that it's working. When people are getting a clear message from you, they will begin to treat you more respectfully.

Learning to speak clearly and give a clear message is what we call 'owning your personal power.' Owning your personal power means you are taking back your right to decide for yourself what kind of life you want to choose. What happens in dysfunctional families is that we grow up forgetting that we have any personal rights. Because of the way we were treated in our families, we learn to tolerate anything in the name of love.

Disrespectful people don't give you respect unless they can see that you respect yourself. You have to know from the inside out that you absolutely don't have to tolerate anything less than love and respect. If you want to accomplish that, you have to speak very clearly and emphatically. In other words, as long as you tolerate disrespect or abuse, you will get it. *So, the bottom line is that it's a complete waste of your time and energy to sit around blaming others for how poorly they treat you. They will treat you that way as long as you allow it. When you stop allowing it, they will stop doing it.*

It's true that you are risking losing a relationship when you tell them you are no longer willing to be disrespected or abused. The question you must ask your self is whether a disrespectful or abusive relationship is worth saving, if the other person really doesn't care about your feelings or your needs? Is that the kind of world you really want to live in? I've found in my experience that most people will stick around and respect you more over time when you do own your power. The few who fall away will actually improve your world by their absence.

It's not necessary to be mean, hateful, nasty, or disrespectful when you set clear boundaries. On the contrary, you can be very kind, but you do have to make sure there is no double message in your voice when you speak. Otherwise, the person you're speaking to will still be chuckling under their breath. When your voice is not clear and strong, they know that they are still in control, even though you may think differently.

It's normal when you first start setting boundaries to do it all wrong before you learn to do it right. Don't give up if that happens to you! You won't usually go from being wimpy to being kind, calm and assertive in one jump. Generally you'll go through a stage of feeling like everything you say is coming out wrong and every one in your life is angry and upset with you. If that's what you're experiencing, don't give up! It's much better to do it wrong than not do it at all. Once you've started owning your power, you can then take the next step of learning how to do it with kindness.

Just remember that you're not finished with this boundaries project until you can set clear boundaries with love and kindness. One way to do that is to put yourself in the other person's shoes and think of how you can set the boundary in a way that is kind and considerate of their feelings as well as your own. It takes time to master that skill, but if you hang in there, I am confident you'll learn how to do it!

I know that owning your power and setting clear boundaries is a lot to think about. I don't expect you to get it perfect in one day, or even one week or one month. All I ask is that you do some soul searching about who it is in your life that you are still allowing to use and abuse you, and then start practicing saying "No!" in front of the mirror on a daily basis. In time, you'll find yourself spontaneously saying "No!" to the people whom you allowed to abuse you previously.

So let's get to work. You're going to be amazed at the difference this makes in your life. You can actually create a world full of love and support all around you. When you take back your power, stop tolerating disrespect and abuse, and learn to set clear, strong boundaries, it gets so much easier to feel joy and light-heartedness, because you're so much happier with yourself and your life!

Homework Assignment: Chapter Nine

1. Make a list of the people in your life who still abuse you or disrespect you today.

2. With each one, write a paragraph about what you do that allows the disrespect or abuse to go on, and a second paragraph about what you could do differently to own your power and set clear boundaries about what you will and will not tolerate.

3. Stand in front of the mirror today and tomorrow for at least a half-hour and practice at least 100 different ways of saying "No!" Keep your hand over your belly button and practice speaking clearly and emphatically from your gut!

4. Keep a record in your journal for the next couple of weeks of how things are changing in your life as a result of setting clear boundaries.

5. When someone does not respect the boundary you set, write in your daily journal about what you did that gave a double message and how you could be clearer and more emphatic in the future.

6. If you'd like to learn more about setting boundaries in verbally or emotionally abusive relationships, there are a few books that might be very helpful:
   The Verbally Abusive Relationship, by Patricia Evans
   The Emotionally Abusive Relationship, by Beverly Engel
   No More Mr. Nice Guy, a book for men, by Dr.. Wes A. Glover

7. Write a few pages about how you feel after doing today's homework.

Good job! Doesn't that feel wonderful? Your whole life is going to be changing for the better, because you are finally realizing that you have the power to create the loving, harmonious life that you want by setting clear boundaries about what you don't want! I'm so proud of you! Keep up the good work!

Chapter Ten

Discover Who You Really Are, Appreciate Yourself, and Make Time To Do What You Love!

Susan

Susan's parents were divorced when she was only a year old so she had no recollection of a father figure. When she was small, her family consisted of her mother, an older brother and an older sister. Susan's mother took very good care of her children, sewed beautiful clothes, played games and cards with them and volunteered as their Campfire leader, but she was not an openly emotional person.

Susan grew up feeling like her father didn't care about his children and her mother was too busy raising kids to worry about their emotional well being. She says her mother had her own emotional pain. Susan learned at a very early age that food was her source of comfort when she was feeling badly. When she married, she picked a partner that was strong and provided financial security, but he, too, was emotionally unavailable, so food again became her comfort.

Being a people pleaser, Susan always wanted to do what made everyone happy so they would like her. She was very good at stuffing her own feelings of sadness and lack of self-worth. She spent thirty years trying to please everyone else and always feeling like a failure. She and her husband raised two wonderful children, but still Susan never felt like she was quite good enough. She felt a deep sadness inside, but she blamed herself for it. Life just had a big gray cloud over it.

The process of emotional healing was amazing for Susan. At first she felt so much anger and rage for all the years she had lost believing in her failures, shortcomings and inadequacies. It felt so wonderful to find that she was okay and that she was a good person who did the very best she knew. Susan learned that she could change the way things were rather than just tolerating everything. She began to realize how she had enabled others to treat her poorly. She said it felt wonderful to stand up for her self and set clear boundaries. Owning her personal power was an overwhelming feeling for Susan because she had spent fifty years feeling totally powerless.

In therapy Susan realized that she never talked about her own life and that she didn't really know anything about herself. For so many years, she felt like she was someone's housekeeper, someone's mother, or someone's wife. She had completely lost herself years ago and getting to know her self was frightening. She didn't know what she enjoyed, what she was capable of doing or where she wanted to go. She says she felt like she didn't have a functional brain of her own. When I gave her a college class booklet to look through one day, she was totally amazed at the things that peaked her interest.

Now Susan realizes that her family is the most important thing in the world to her. She says her children and grandchildren bring her incredible joy. She says she wants to learn to share that joy with her husband because they both feel very strongly about their family. Susan loves to garden and she loves to arrange beautiful flowers to enjoy their beauty. She loves doing things with her hands like knitting, sewing, creating handmade cards, or scrap-booking. She enjoys remodeling and redecorating her home to create a warm, cozy, inviting environment. She adores animals and can't imagine life without them.

Today Susan says her life is very different than it was before. She used to think that if only she had worked harder, been prettier, thinner, or smarter, people would treat her better. She has a much happier outlook on life today. She no longer blames herself for everything negative that happens around her. She no longer lets anyone control what she thinks or does, and she is now able to defend her thoughts and opinions. Susan says she feels free today to insist that she absolutely be treated with love and respect. She feels proud of who she is and she enjoys the life she has created for herself.

Days 19 and 20

Hello again! How are you today? Are you feeling strong and powerful? Great! Isn't that a good feeling? I'm so happy that you're practicing the things we're talking about, because I know without a doubt that when you do that over time, your life will change dramatically. So are you having fun yet? How cool! Me too. I love seeing people get better. You have no idea how much it's going to help you over time. You're going to be so happy that you took this journey!

Today we start getting to the fun stuff! We're going to find out who you really are inside all that crazy, dysfunctional family wrapping that you've been wearing all your life. I'm excited! I love this part of therapy. I've had lots of clients ask me in the past, "What if I find out who I am and I don't like myself?" In case you have that fear, let me tell you that in twenty-five years of working with people, it has never happened. Every person who has taken the time to undo the emotional damage has found someone very special and wonderful inside. I know that you will too. So let's get started.

So here's another million-dollar question. I want you to ask yourself "Who am I?" Are you the fear and anxiety that you've been carrying around for a lifetime? Are you the depression that you've never been able to overcome? Are you the timid, little person who shivers in your shoes and let's people control you? Or are you the angry, acting out monster that you've become in the past when someone crossed your boundaries? Who are you?

Often we've been so busy just trying to survive that we've never taken the time to get to know who we really are. We're too busy, or too stressed, or we just don't have time, or whatever our current excuse may be, we just don't want to find out what's inside of us. Sometimes, like I said, we're afraid that our inner self might be a monster of some kind and that we won't like the person we find. Relax! It's not going to be that bad. Finding yourself is actually an exciting adventure. Remember when you were a kid and you went on adventures that were scary and fun? This is one of those scary, *fun* adventures. Actually it's not very scary at all, now that you're an adult, but it definitely is a lot of fun.

Let's start by thinking about what you like about yourself. I'd like you to start by thinking of at least three talents, qualities or abilities you have that you appreciate. For example, maybe you are kind, or caring, or considerate of others. Maybe you love deeply, or you make people laugh, or maybe you have the talent of seeing the good in everyone. I'm sure you have some wonderful qualities and talents and abilities! Just think about it for a minute, and I know they'll come floating to your mind.

If it's a struggle to think of three things you like or appreciate about yourself, I'd like you to play a little game with me. I want you to think of someone you love and imagine that you could see yourself through his or her eyes. If the person you love was writing a letter about you, what positive words would they say about you? Would they talk about your honesty, your integrity or your sense of humor? Would they remember the times you took time out of your life to be there for them in some way? I want you to take a minute and really think about what the people you love might appreciate about you.

Sometimes it really helps to see ourselves through the eyes of people who love us. If we experienced a lot of criticism or abuse in our lives, it can be a challenge to see the good in ourselves. The good news is, everyone has wonderful God-given talents and abilities, *even you!* You just have to take the time to bring them out of hiding and focus on them.

So now I'd like you another imaginary game. I want you to imagine that you have a friend who has those same good qualities that we just discovered in you. Would you value a person who had qualities like that in your life? Would you value and honor them and want to be close to them? If you'd appreciate those qualities in your friend, why not take a few moments and really appreciate them in yourself? Let yourself relax for a few moments and really enjoy the feeling of valuing and appreciating you.

Often we spend so much time thinking about what's wrong with us, that we never take time to appreciate what's right. We take ourselves for granted and we look for others to value and appreciate us when we are not valuing and appreciating ourselves.

Remember our discussions about the unconscious mind? Well, here's another thing to remember about the unconscious. When we don't value and appreciate ourselves, our unconscious mind draws people into our lives who reflect to us the negative way we feel about ourselves. But when we do value and appreciate ourselves, our unconscious mind attracts people to us who also value and appreciate us.

Maybe you were taught as a child that appreciating yourself was being egotistical. Many of us heard that when we were children, but the opposite is actually true. People who are egotistical don't love themselves. That's why they are always trying to convince everyone else how special or important they are.

When you really love and appreciate yourself, you don't have to tell the whole world about it because you feel good from the inside out. It becomes obvious to everyone else that you are a healthy, happy person, because the love you have for yourself actually bubbles over into unconditional love for everyone else around you.

Okay, let's move on. Discovering who you really are also involves paying attention to your feelings throughout the day, and noticing what feels good to you and what doesn't. When you pay attention, you get signals from yourself that tell you what you enjoy doing and what you don't enjoy, or who you enjoy spending time with and who you don't.

Often when we grew up in dysfunctional families, we learned to ignore or tune out our own signals, and to listen instead for what other people approved of. Instead of paying attention to our own signals, we learned to pay attention to what everyone else thought was important. Often we were so busy trying to determine what they wanted or approved of, that we forget to focus on what really mattered to us.

Do you remember from our discussions earlier that the term 'co-dependent' refers to people who grew up in dysfunctional families? Well, here's another definition for you; this one says it even better. The humorous definition of a codependent is this; you can call yourself a 'codependent' if when you're drowning, someone else's life flashes before your eyes!

Yes, that definition is very cute, but it could also be quite sad when you stop and think about it. What it really means is that we codependents often make someone else the center of our lives. We don't know how to be the center of our own life, because our entire childhood was spent reacting to someone else's feelings and needs instead of listening to our own.

We don't know what we feel, or what we need or want, because we are so busy trying to please other people in the hopes that maybe this time we'll be loved. Sometimes it gets so bad that we even choose our careers based on what our parents or our families think we should do instead of basing our decision on what we, ourselves, are interested in.

Does any of this ring true for you? If you are one of those 'need-less, want-less codependents' that doesn't know who you are, it's time you start reclaiming who you really are. I know you can do it, because I've helped many other people do it in the past. The first step is to begin paying attention on a daily basis to those little signals you get from yourself throughout the day.

If you want to know yourself, it's very important to notice what feels good to you and what doesn't. You can pay attention to the people you enjoy being around and those you don't enjoy. You'll also want to notice which activities you enjoy doing and which ones you don't enjoy. What's really fun is to notice what excites you, what makes you feel passionate and alive, and what fascinates you so much that you just can't get enough of it!

If you start keeping these things in your awareness, you can begin to make decisions based on your own feelings and your own desires. For example, if you have noticed that one particular friend who calls you every day always leaves you feeling bad after every conversation, you could choose not to talk to that friend today.

You could use the boundaries process we learned yesterday to let them know when would be a good time for you to talk to them, if there is a good time You may find in time that you don't actually want that person as a friend, but don't worry about that right now. Just start with trusting yourself today, and making a decision today about what feels good to you and what doesn't.

Let's try another example. Suppose someone invites you to lunch and asks you where you would like to go. Instead of saying, "I don't care," like you usually do, you could think about the places you know that you have enjoyed in the past and actually choose a restaurant that sounds good to you.

Or let's say you have a day off and that little nagging voice inside your mind says you really should be cleaning your house so that it looks good when your friends come to visit. Instead of giving in to the nagging voice that wants you to do what others expect of you, why not ask yourself, "What do I really want to do today?"

Maybe cleaning the house feels important to you deep inside or maybe it doesn't. Or maybe you could clean for an hour or two and then have the rest of the day to do things that you really want to do. The important thing to remember is to pay attention to your own feelings. If you pay attention, you will know what is right for you.

So let's get to work. Smile! We've got homework to do!

Homework Assignment: Chapter Ten

1. Think of at least three things you like about yourself and write them down. If that's difficult for you, I'd like you to write a letter to yourself from someone you love. This letter is going to be about what this person appreciates about you. Really think about what they would appreciate, and write it in detail.

2. Now I'd like you to imagine having a friend like you, and write about what you would appreciate about a friend who has those wonderful qualities and abilities you just discovered in yourself. Would you value and appreciate a friend like that?

3. Now take a moment to really appreciate your self and write a paragraph about how that feels. What is that like for you?

4. Write a paragraph about how your negative feelings about yourself in the past have affected other's opinions of you. Did you put yourself down so much that the people in your life learned to take you for granted? How could you start valuing yourself more, so that others would value you too?

5. Now let's answer some easy questions:
    a. What is your favorite color?
    b. What is your favorite music?
    c. What is your favorite time of day? Why?
    d. What is your favorite season of the year? Why?
    e. What was the best year of your life? Why?

6. So let's go on to the next level:
    a. What kind of house would you live in if you could choose what you want without worrying about money or about other people's opinions?
    b. What kind of car would you drive if you had plenty of money and didn't have to consider other people's opinions?

    c. What kind of work would you do, if money or other people's needs and wants didn't matter?

7. Now let's focus first on what you do outside of work. I'd like you to make a list of the people you normally spend time with, the activities you normally do in a week, and the way you spend your time. So here we go:

    a. Who do you normally spend your time with?

    b. What do you normally do in your time off work?

    c. What activities do you participate in on a regular basis?

8. Okay, so now, let's write about what you would do if you could do what you really want to do:

    a. Who would you choose to spend time with if you could do what you wanted?

    b. What would you do in your time off work if you did what you wanted to do?

    c. What activities would you participate in if you were doing what you wanted?

9. So now I'd like you to write a paragraph about your own personal reasons for spending your time doing what other people want instead of doing what you want. Are these reasons still valid for you, now that you see the truth about them?

10. So here comes the fun part: let's write about your dreams and desires!

    a. What have you always wanted to do in your life but never found a way?

    b. What have you always wanted to learn more about and never had the time, energy, or money?

    c. What fascinates you every time you hear about it, like that feeling that you just can't ever do enough of it or learn enough about it?

11. Please write a paragraph about what you could start doing differently right now to include more of what you like or what interests you in

your life and less of what pleases everyone else.

12. Now I'd like you to gather some old magazines, a poster board, a scissors, and a glue stick, because you're going to create a 'Treasure Map.' You may think you still don't know much about what you want in your life, but if you simply start paging through the old magazines and look for pictures and words that attract you, you'll be amazed at how much you already know about what you want!

So your homework is to cut out words and pictures that show images or feelings of what you want to bring into your life in the next year, and then make a collage on the poster board of the words and images you've chosen. Somewhere in the middle of your collage I want you to put a picture of yourself, as well as a word or image that signifies your Higher Power.

You see, you are going to create the 'Treasure Map,' but your Higher Power is responsible for bringing these things in to your life. Your job is to look at it daily so that it gets programmed into your unconscious mind, and trust your Higher Power to do the rest.

When you've created your masterpiece, hang the collage somewhere where you will see it everyday, because even if you don't look at it consciously, your unconscious mind will take it in and it will begin to bring those things about in your life.

13. Okay, you're almost done! Now I'd just like you to write a few pages about how you feel after doing today's homework.

Hey, great job! Isn't this fun? Don't forget to congratulate yourself. You should be very proud of yourself for all your hard work and your progress!

Chapter Eleven

Relax, Be Grateful, and Use Your Imagination to Create What You Want!

Kate

Kate grew up as one of four children on a farm in the Midwest. Her father developed Parkinson's disease when Kate was two and he was ill until his death when she was fifteen. She and her siblings were taught to work hard, to live austerely, and to "bear the cross" they had been given. Denial reigned strong and they never talked about the their father's incapacitating illness. It was an "elephant in the living room"

Because of her Dad's illness, Kate's oldest brother became physically and sexually abusive. He held a lot of power in the family as the oldest son. Kate was deeply hurt by her brother's abuse, but like most children in dysfunctional families, she had no way to resolve the emotional pain.

When she grew up and left home, Kate married an emotionally and verbally abusive alcoholic. He was clinically depressed, he smoked heavily and he was also addicted to television. Kate was codependent at the time and her husband provided a bottomless pit of neediness that she constantly tried to fill. Although she knew he was alcoholic, she did her best to live a life of normalcy in the world. It was much like her childhood. She was miserable and lonely, still "bearing her cross."

Soon after they were married, she and her husband began alcohol recovery work. Her husband went through six treatment programs before their marriage ended. Kate became deeply involved in Al-Anon for many years. It was there she first began her emotional healing journey. Reconnecting with a sense of spirituality, working the steps, and sharing her growth with others were the basic parts of her Al-Anon group.

Kate says that learning to surrender her will was a magnificent turning point in her life. She remembers sitting on the rim of the city looking out at the clouds and finally giving up her picture of how things should or could be, and then turning her life over to the Higher Power. Still today, she says that surrender continues to be a core of her spiritual walk through life.

Kate and I met when she chose to do psychotherapy to resolve the emotional pain of her childhood. She says the emotional healing she did with me helped her to see the patterns in her life and to feel—really feel. As she healed her childhood issues, Kate began to yearn for a different kind of life. She was a career woman at that time, but somewhere deep inside she had always wanted to have a family of her own.

I taught Kate to use the power of her imagination to manifest the life she really wanted. She was very doubtful at first and quite convinced that no matter how much she visualized that there were simply no good men in the world who could provide her an opportunity for family. At thirty-nine years old, she didn't have much time left to have her own children. I remember telling Kate that she didn't have to find a lot of good men; all she really needed was one. I suggested that if she could stretch her mind to believe even for a moment that there could be one good man available to her, I was sure that the Universe would provide.

Kate met her new husband at one of my personal growth workshops. They started a friendship that developed over time. Before long, they were very happily married. At their wedding I sang "Love Can Build a Bridge," and a few other songs that spoke to the beauty and depth of their love.

Kate's life today looks very different than before. She has beautiful twin daughters; a kind, gentle stepson; a loving, devoted husband and a rich spiritual life in both the Sufi path and also the Quaker tradition. She has also recently completed her doctorate by writing a dissertation on bringing the path of heart into the field of education. She continues to hold her spiritual focus and she gives thanks daily with the prayer "Oh, thou the Sustainer of our bodies, hearts, and souls, bless all that we receive in thankfulness."

Days 21 and 22

Hi there! How are you today? Are you enjoying yourself? Do you feel like you have a better sense of who you are and what you want? Great! We're making good progress! Today we're going to work on how to bring your dreams into reality in your life. Are you saying, "Yeah, sure," like you really don't believe me? That's okay. I'm not asking for blind faith. I'm just asking that you try some of these new ideas that I'm offering you and then see for yourself what works for you. Is that fair?

The first thing we're going to do today is to check and make sure that you are physically relaxed. The way you know that you are relaxed is when all the muscles in your body are loose and there's no tension anywhere. Sometimes we get tense just from trying to get things done and dealing with all the different responsibilities and expectations in our lives. But more often, when our bodies are tense or tight, it's because we have some feelings stored up in our unconscious mind that we need to deal with.

So before we go any further, I'd like you to check in with yourself and see if there are feelings you need to deal with today before you move forward with being thankful and using your imagination to bring your dreams into reality. If you have feelings that are stirred up inside, I'd suggest you go back to Chapter Three and work through the feelings. When there is tension in your body, your unconscious mind is not clear to be thankful or to create good things in your life.

Okay! So if you are truly relaxed, let's spend a little time thinking about what you are thankful for in your life. Being thankful or grateful is the first step to creating good things in your life. If you don't appreciate the good you already have, God will not give you more. So I don't want you to skim over this part like "Oh, sure, I'm thankful for my health, and my job, and my home, and my family, so what's next?" That's not true gratitude; that's lip service! I want you to put your heart into being grateful, by reflecting sincerely on what you appreciate the most about your life today.

So I'd like you to think about you are thankful for that has really touched your heart recently. Sometimes they are little things, like a special moment with a child that you love, or the loving support of someone who cares about you when you are having a difficult time, or the incredible natural beauty you see on your drive to work in the morning. Yes, I'd also like you to include your partner, and your family, and your job, and your home, but instead of just quickly listing them, I'd like you to think about what you really value about each of those things. What makes them a true gift in your life?

Now, I'd like you to sit and feel the energy of true gratitude for a moment. How does it feel to you? Generally it's a very pleasant, uplifting feeling that brings a positive energy with it. If you're not experiencing that yet, then you may need to focus a bit more on what you're truly grateful for in your life. Just let yourself feel the warm glow of true gratitude. It's a very lovely state of mind to hang out in.

I'd suggest that if you really want to experience fun and lightheartedness in your life, that you practice hanging out in the "attitude of gratitude" every day for a period of time. Make it a daily habit that you do at a particular time in your day. Every morning on your way to work you could think about what you are most grateful for in your life, or every night before you go to sleep you could write down several things that you are especially grateful for. You'll be amazed at how your life changes just by doing that simple process.

Now comes the fun part! Are you ready? Okay! Here we go! When you're in this attitude of gratitude it becomes much easier to use your unconscious mind to create more good things in your life. All you have to do is think of something you really want and then imagine already having it, as if that was true right now. Your imagination is one of the most powerful natural abilities you have when you learn to utilize your power.

Think about the fact that every building that stands in the town you live in was once just an idea in someone's imagination. Every business that was started there was once someone's idea that they believed in and started working towards. Every house that was built was once someone's idea of a home they were creating for their family or their loved ones. People bring their dreams into reality every day.

So what dreams do you have that you want to manifest in your physical world? Do you want a new car or a new job? Do you want a loving partner? Do you want a beautiful home to come home to at night after you've finished your day's work? What feels important to you? What do you want more than anything in the world?

Okay, so here's the secret about manifesting your dreams into reality. *If you want something more than anything in the world, then imagine that you already have it! Imagine your self living it, and breathing it, and enjoying it, and being so very grateful that it finally arrived.* Imagine the joy that would come from this wonderful addition to your life. Imagine telling your friends about it and having them be excited for you that it finally came true. If you really want something, spend five or ten minutes every day just loving the feeling of having what you want and feeling grateful for it from the bottom of your heart!

What often happens when people try to create a new reality is that they get caught up in what they don't want rather than on what they want. They spend so much time and energy thinking about what's wrong with their lives that there's no time and energy left to think about having what they want. So, please listen carefully, because here's where the magic comes. *The way your subconscious mind works is that whatever you focus on, you get more of!* If you focus on what you don't want, you'll get more of that. But if you turn your focus to what you really want, and hang out with the feeling of having it, you'll be amazed at how it finds a way to show up in your life.

Your feelings are very important in this process. It's not enough just to visualize having what you want and seeing the pictures in your mind of you driving the new car, or you living in the new house. You have to actually feel yourself already there. How would it feel if your dreams were reality? *The secret of manifesting is to hang out in the feeling of already having what you want and loving every minute of it!* That's where the joy and light-heartedness comes, in imagining the feeling of your life the way you really want it to be.

Lynn Grabhorn, in her book *Excuse Me, Your life is Waiting* has a trusty little exercise that helps you stay on track. It helps you focus on what you want rather than on what you don't want, and then focus on the feeling of actually having it. There are four steps to the exercise.

First, you ask yourself, *"What is it that I don't want?"* Give yourself time to really focus on your answer before you go on. Next ask yourself: *"What is it that I do want?"* Again, give yourself plenty of time to focus and answer. The third question is: *"What benefits would I receive in my life from having what I want?"* Let yourself have fun with this and really imagine having those benefits as you focus on them! And the fourth question is this: *"How would I feel if I got what I wanted?"*

To really get the benefit of this exercise, you'll want to hang out in the feeling of having what you want as long as you can, because that's the most powerful step in the process. If you walk yourself through this exercise a few times, you'll see how beautifully it works. It's very powerful for getting you motivated and on track.

A great way to use this exercise is to do it with a friend. Have your friend ask you the four questions and you answer them, and then switch roles and you ask the questions and have your friend answer them. You can cover lots of areas in your life, but just imagine them one at a time. When you get to the question of how it would feel to have what you want, you can both visualize for each other the beautiful feeling of having what you want.

Years ago, one of my friends and I used this little exercise when we went walking together in the evenings after work. We'd take turns asking each other the questions, over and over, throughout our three-mile walk. We loved doing it because we both got very high and lighthearted just from doing the exercise.

Interestingly enough, among many other things that actually came true in our lives as a result of our visualizing together, we both met our life partners within a year from that time. It's amazing how powerfully our lives can change for the better when we simply take the time to do something so simple.

Manifesting your dreams into reality is one of the most fun parts of getting healthy, because you never know how the Higher Power will bring those dreams into reality. God has a great sense of humor and He does it so much better than we ever could! Often you may struggle and strain on your own trying desperately to make something happen, and then when you finally let go and let God be in charge, it manifests effortlessly and beautifully.

Your part is to keep focusing on the dream as if it's already true for five minutes every day, and then surrender and let the Higher Power be in charge of the actual manifestation. *You will be guided through your intuition to do what you need to do to be at the right place at the right time to bring your dreams into reality.* It is important that you remember to pay attention to what your intuition is trying to get through to you.

Remember that your intuition is that gut feeling inside you that tells you what to do next, even when it doesn't make sense to you logically. For example, maybe you're looking for a new job and you've gone through all the steps to imagine your dream job. You may have done everything you know to do to bring it about, but nothing has shown up yet. Then one day you have a gut feeling that says "I think I need to visit Mary today," and when you go to Mary's house, you *just happen* to bump into an old friend of hers that *just happens* to know of the perfect job for you. We call it 'coincidence,' but actually it's the Higher Power guiding us through our intuition to bring our dreams into reality.

Some things you imagine will come true very quickly sometimes even within twenty-four hours. Others may take years, depending on your own beliefs about yourself and your own worthiness, and your unconscious willingness to receive what you are focusing on.

If something you really want is not manifesting quickly enough for you, I'd suggest that you go back to Chapter Five and work on changing any negative beliefs you have about yourself and your worthiness that could stand in the way of you receiving what you want. *Negative beliefs about yourself or your own worthiness will counteract your ability to manifest your dreams.* You may also need to go back to Chapter Seven and work on forgiving anyone who you have not totally forgiven. *The lack of forgiveness towards anyone stops the flow of life in you and also keeps your dreams from manifesting.*

So let's do some homework! You're going to love manifesting your dreams. This is the beginning of a whole new life. When you bring your dreams into reality, your whole world is going to change dramatically for the better!

Homework Assignment: Chapter Eleven

1. First I'd like you to check in with your body to see if your body is relaxed. If you can take a few deep breaths, and think about relaxing your body, and bring yourself back to a state of relaxation, then go ahead with today's homework. Otherwise, go back to Chapter Three and work through the feelings that are keeping your body tense and tight before you attempt to do today's homework.

    Don't worry! You're going to get there either way! If this book takes you 90 days instead of 33, it will be well worth your time and effort! How many years did it take you to get to this point in your life? A whole new start on your life is worth every minute you put into it!

2. Now, I'd like you to list at least ten things in your life that you feel deeply grateful for. Remember not to do this half-heartedly! If you want to feel the attitude of gratitude, you have to put your heart and soul in to it. Think about things that have really touched you in the past few days or the past few weeks and write them down very specifically. Notice how you feel when you are truly grateful.

3. Hey, you're doing great! Now we're going to focus on what other

wonderful, magical people, or situations, or things you want to bring into your life. I'd like you to list at least ten things that you really want to manifest in your life that would make your life even better than it is today. Write them down very specifically. Remember to be careful what you ask for!

I've talked to lots of people who have done this process who got exactly what they asked for. Keep that in mind when you're visualizing your dreams. If you leave out important parts, you may have to go back to the drawing board after it manifests and do it over again.

4.   Now I'd like you to pick the three most important things on your list, and one-by-one, I'd like you to go a little bit more in depth. I'd like you to do the exercise we talked about today from Lynn Grabhorn's book. The exercise goes like this:

1. Focus on what you don't want in this area of your life.
2. Focus on what you do want.
3. Focus on the benefits you would receive from having what you want in your life.
4. Now focus on how you would feel if you got what you wanted. Let yourself enjoy hanging out in this feeling of having what you want for as long as you can before you go on!

   For each of the three things you are focusing on, please write a paragraph about that incredible feeling of having what you want!

5.   Write a paragraph about your willingness to surrender and let God be in charge of manifesting your dreams into reality. In the past, have you ever experienced the difference between trying to do it yourself or letting God be in charge? If so, write about your experience.

6.   Now write a paragraph about your willingness to pay attention and follow your intuition, even when it doesn't make sense logically. Do you understand that the Higher Power is guiding you through your intuition to bring your dreams into reality? Have you had any intu-

itions recently that you have not been following?

7. If you want to give yourself that extra boost towards manifesting what you want more quickly, I'd suggest that you go back and review Chapter Five on changing your negative beliefs about yourself, and then review Chapter Seven on forgiving anyone in your life who you have not completely forgiven.

8. There are three books that I'd recommend if you want to learn more about manifesting abundance in your life. They are:
   Creative Visualization, by Shakti Gawain.
   Excuse Me, Your Life Is Waiting, by Lynn Grabhorn.
   Ask and It Is Given, by Esther and Jerry Hicks.

9. To complete today's homework, I'd like you to write a few pages about how you feel after doing the homework processes today.

Hey, great job! I'm so proud of you for completing this! Be sure you're ready for the change that's coming, because your life is definitely going to change for the better!

Chapter Twelve

Live Your Spirituality and Ask for Divine Help!

Daniel

Daniel grew up as one of seven children in an American missionary family. Daniel's parents were sent by his church to save the souls of the "heathen" in Africa. He describes his parents as "wonderfully dysfunctional" because they were always giving love to others, but they never learned how to receive that love in return.

From a young age, Daniel role-modeled after his parents, giving and giving everything he had to others until all that was left of him was an empty shell. Because there was no hospital for hundreds of miles from their African home, Daniel and his mother cared for sick people day and night, wrapping broken bones and holding dying children in their arms. Daniel's young life grew even more confusing when at only age eleven, he was sexually abused by a minister in his church.

The dysfunctional pattern of giving and giving and never receiving carried into Daniel's adult life. He married first an alcoholic and then a rage-aholic. Like Daniel's parents, his wives were not able to be emotionally available for him. Daniel thought if he only gave enough, he could heal his partner's emotional wounds, but when he tried to accomplish that, he lost himself.

Although he dreamed of having a loving family with happy children, his codependent choices made that impossible.

Daniel started emotional healing out of despair. He was ready to leave a therapy session one day when his therapist asked, "Why are you always putting yourself in relationships where you can never be loved?" Although his hand was already on the doorknob, Daniel chose to stay and face his inner demons.

Years later, Daniel and I worked together in therapy to help him feel and release the pain of his childhood wounds and learn to value himself as much as he valued others. It was challenging for Daniel to learn to love him self and very difficult for him to ask others for love and support. Little by little, he began doing things to treat him self with love, like buying fresh flowers to put on his dining room table and allowing healthy, supportive relationships to enter his life.

Daniel met the beautiful woman who would be his life-partner at one of my personal growth workshops. Intuitively he knew that with her he could find a place where his intellect, his creativity, and his heart could be open, but still he was terrified! He worked through his fear and saw that this was indeed a woman with whom he could let down his guard. Today, Daniel has found the intimacy he always believed deep in his heart was possible. His partner has become a great teacher and companion.

Two and a half years ago, Daniel was diagnosed with prostate cancer and given less than a twenty-five percent chance to live. Instead of following the doctor's orders, Daniel began an intense journey to heal himself by taking love and light into every cell of his body every day. He described the process of healing as a prayer practice that required that he breathe deeply and quiet his mind from the demands of the world. He described it as entering the quiet and holy place where in stillness he allowed Divine Presence to speak to him. In this place, he found guidance of what he needed to be doing to regain his health.

Today Daniel is still healing and growing. He says he has learned to trust God after many years of running away from God in anger. In the process of opening his heart, he says that the Divine Presence brought healing to his body, mind, and spirit. Today, Daniel is also doing work in the world that brings him great joy and engages him in service to others.

Daniel believes that the spiritual journey calls for living in the present instead of carrying the woundedness of the past or living in fear of what the future might bring. He describes it as being totally at peace inside, while having a willingness to be an instrument of God's love right now in the present moment.

Days 23 and 24

Hello again! How are you today? Does it feel like you got on a very fast-moving train and you're speeding through the countryside at a hundred miles an hour? That's okay! I know it's a lot of information to digest, but you wanted the short course, didn't you? You could do it the long, slow way, like I did, and take thirty years to learn what I'm teaching you, but thanks to the age of technology, even personal growth can come on the fast train these days!

I think that you and I are having fun together, so let's just keep moving forward! Is that okay with you? If it gets too overwhelming, it's okay to slow down and spend more time on any of these chapters, or come back to them over and over throughout your life until you get them right. There are no rules for growth; you just do it in your own way and your own time until you really "get it" at a gut level. Trust me, you will know from the inside out when you feel better!

So our topic today is living your spirituality and asking for divine help. Remember that spirituality is different from traditional religion. Traditional religion is about dogma and belief systems, and someone else's idea about life after death, and about what it takes to get to heaven when you die. I once heard a joke that said traditional religion is for people who are afraid of going to hell and spirituality is for people who have already been there. Most of us know the feeling of living in hell right here on earth. To me, spirituality is about living your life in such a way that you create a life that feels like heaven on earth.

When I was a child, I grew up in a church where people talked about God and religion all the time and tried to convince others to believe the way they did, because they honestly believed that they had the only way to get to heaven. Like many others, it was a religion that was based on fear, and guilt, and control, and sad to say, it also included a lot of hypocrisy and abuse behind the scenes.

As a result, I grew up so confused about God that by the time I left home I never wanted to hear the word 'God' again. I was very frustrated with the hypocrisy of the belief system. It was later, through my own emotional healing process, that I found a new understanding of God. Now I know that God really is love, like I was originally taught as a child. But I also understand now that the people who hurt me in the church were people who had their own emotional pain and didn't have the psychological tools we now have for healing that pain.

Because of my own difficult religious experience, I believe that it's very important that we allow each other to have our own belief systems, whatever they are. We can share our spirituality, which is our direct connection to God, and we can support each other in our spiritual growth, but we need to let other people have their own opinion about who and what God really is.

I also believe that it's much more important to live our beliefs rather than just talking about them. All the talk in the world doesn't change the way we treat someone when the chips are down. We have to learn to walk our talk, and put our beliefs into action on a daily basis if we want to reap the true rewards of a spiritual life. When we live our spirituality daily, we can honestly get to the point where we feel happy and lighthearted on a regular basis. Living our spirituality naturally brings us joy and lightheartedness.

So, how can you live your spirituality? The first step to living your spirituality on a daily basis is simply to know that there is a Power greater than you that wants you to be happy and wants you to have a good life. When you acknowledge this Higher Power in your life, then you can call on it and ask for help and guidance at any time, with anything you are facing.

You don't have to kneel and pray to build a relationship with God. You can simply talk to God in your mind, like you would talk to a good friend. When something is challenging you and you don't know what to do, say a prayer in your mind and ask for help and guidance. Or if you need help in some area and you don't have anyone in your life who can help you, say a prayer and ask for divine help.

You'll be surprised and amazed at how the answers will come! Sometimes books will jump off the shelves that have the perfect solution to your challenge, or people show up in your life that know exactly how to guide you through whatever it is that your are facing. It's very fun to watch all the creative ways that God and his angels find to bring us solutions to our problems and challenges!

You see, there are thousands of unemployed angels just waiting to help you! When you ask God for help, God delegates angels to help you and guide you in whatever way you need. Our biggest problem is that we often forget to ask. Because of our experiences in dysfunctional families in which our needs and wants were not important, we think that we have to do everything ourselves, so too often we forget to ask!

I could tell you hundreds of stories of all the ways I have been helped and guided when I asked for Divine help. The ways the answers come never cease to amaze me. God obviously has a good sense of humor. Many times I end up laughing at the incredible ways God has to answer my prayers. Try it for yourself! You'll find out from your own experience what I'm talking about. It's very fun to see God working in your life. If you think about it, even reading this book may have been the answer to a powerful, silent prayer for help and guidance that you had in your heart.

The next step of living your spirituality is to live a life of honesty and integrity. If you think about it, you can tie up a lot of your valuable energy in negative ways if you lie, and cheat, and use people, and then spend your time arguing and trying to defend yourself about who was right or wrong. What an incredible waste of energy that is! If you live that way, you will never get what you really want. Even if you make a million dollars, you'll still end up lonely and depressed. You'll have all that money and no one to genuinely love and support you, let alone someone who wants to laugh and have fun with you. It's hard to have fun all by yourself every day.

It's so much easier to live the golden rule and treat people the way you want to be treated from the start. If you've spent a lot of your life in negative ways up until now, it's not too late to change! Simply forgive yourself for the past, and then start over today and practice living the golden rule from this point on. The golden rule, for those of you who may not remember, is simply the teaching of Jesus Christ, which is to "Love your neighbor as yourself!"

So, living a life of honesty and integrity needs to be the basis that you build on for living your spirituality every day. What that means is you tell the truth, you are honest in your dealings with other people, and you treat them the way you want to be treated. If you own a business, you treat your employees the way you would want to be treated if you were the employee and they owned the business. If you are a parent, you treat your children the way you wish your parents had treated you.

A third step of living your spirituality on a daily basis is really living your life from love. Every religion has a belief that what you give out comes back to you. The Christian Bible says, "What you sow, you shall also reap," or in other words, what you plant in the ground of your life will bear fruit according to what was planted. If you plant disharmony, you will reap disharmony. If you want love to grow in your life, you must plant the seeds of love.

Eastern religions teach the law of karma, which means that the way you live and the way you treat others in this lifetime will affect the lessons you have to learn in the next life. Either way, the truth is the same. What you give out comes back to you. So the bottom line is that before we take any action in our lives, we need to spend time reflecting on what we want to come back to us, and then act accordingly.

If you want love in your life, you'll need to make a conscious effort every day to live your life from love. That means making it your conscious choice to give love to everyone in your life on a regular basis and to always act from love.

Giving love can be done in many ways. Sometimes it's as simple as giving a compliment to someone to let them know you appreciate them or that you enjoy their presence in your life. Sometimes it's taking time to listen and care about the challenges facing another person. You don't need to have the answers to their problems. Sometimes it's giving a hug to show that you care, or sending a supportive card when someone is having a difficult time. Sometimes, when things are going well, it's just taking time to laugh, and play and have fun together.

Another way to live from love is to find a quiet time in your life every day and in this quiet time send love to people. You don't have to be skilled in meditation to send love to others. You can simply lock your door, turn off your phone, and sit in a quiet place where you won't be disturbed. Just imagine yourself out in a beautiful place in nature where you feel close to God and then focus on Divine love pouring through you to everyone in your life.

You can imagine the love being a sparkling light pouring through you in beautiful, radiant colors if you like, or imagine it in any way you enjoy visualizing it. Just take the time to send love to everyone that matters to you in your life and imagine him or her as radiant, healthy and happy.

What works even more powerfully is to send love to anyone you are having problems with in your life. If your children are not behaving the way you think they should, or your boss is being a jerk in your eyes, or your spouse is not giving you the love you think you deserve, take time to send them love every day in your own quiet time. *And please don't say, "Well, I already did that and it didn't work!" Just keep on doing it every day until it does work. Love can heal anything!*

Maybe you need to have an imaginary conversation in your quiet time with the person who is challenging you, and tell them how much you love them and want them to be happy and healthy. Make sure, however, that you don't do all the talking. What may be even more valuable for you is to listen to them in your heart, and let them tell you what is difficult in their lives that is causing them to act in the ways they are acting. Maybe they will also tell you what you are doing that makes life more difficult for them. When you really understand and have compassion for their pain, you'll be amazed at how your relationship with them will change for the better.

The last step in living your spirituality is doing spiritual service in some way in your life. Spiritual service is about giving to others from your heart, like Mother Theresa did when she held beggars in her arms when they were dying. You don't have to give up your entire life to help others like she did, but you could simply make it a point every day to be the unexpected angel in someone else's life. There is an incredible joy that comes from giving from your heart to others who are in need. Sometimes the joy itself is so fulfilling that it's hard to know who enjoys it more, the giver or the receiver!

My favorite prayer through the years has been the prayer of Saint Francis. Some of you may already know it, but for those who don't, let me share it with you. It's unbelievably beautiful! It goes like this:

> "Lord, make me an instrument of your peace;
> where there is hatred, let me sow love;
> where there is injury, pardon;
> where there is doubt, faith;
> where there is despair, hope;
> where there is darkness, light;
> and where there is sadness, joy.
> Oh, Divine Master, grant that I may not so
> much seek to be consoled as to console;
> to be understood as to understand;
> to be loved as to love,
> for it is in giving that we receive,
> it is in pardoning that we are pardoned,
> and it is in dying to self that we are born to eternal life."

Isn't that lovely?

Your own heart will show you where you can best be of service to others. If you had a difficult childhood, maybe you will find a way to give back to children who are hurting today. This may look like volunteering in some organization that cares for abused children, or finding a child that needs help and being the mentor that you wish someone would have been for you when you were young.

If you have a concern about aging, maybe you can find a way to be of service to the elderly, like going to nursing homes and talking to people no one has time to talk to, or taking them out for walks to get some fresh air and see the beauty of nature. There is a natural joy in appreciating the beauty of nature, but the joy multiplies and expands when you share it with someone who is in need.

So let's get to work! Let's take a look at your life and see what changes you could make personally to live your spirituality and ask for divine help. Are you ready?

Homework Assignment: Chapter Twelve

1. What was your experience with spirituality as a child? Write a paragraph or two about what you liked or didn't like about the spirituality you grew up with.

2. Have you ever had an experience of actually getting Divine help when you asked for it? Write about that experience.

3. What are some of the things you would like Divine help on today? Are you asking regularly for that incredible Power of the Universe to help you in your daily life? Write about how you could remind yourself to ask more regularly.

4. Are you living a life of honesty and integrity? Be very honest with yourself! Write a few paragraphs about some of the ways you could live a more pure-hearted, honest life.

5. How do you give love to others on a regular basis? Are there ways you could give more love to the people in your life? How could you be the unexpected angel in other people's lives? Write about some of the ideas that come to you.

6. Do you do any spiritual service regularly? What are some of the ways you have been drawn in the past to doing spiritual service?

Write a paragraph about one or two of those ways you could incorporate this into your life today.

7. Let's do a little meditation. I want you to find a quiet place where you won't be disturbed, and turn off all phones and beepers, and lock the door so no one can interrupt you.

   a. Read through this exercise a couple of times and then sit down and close your eyes and relax deeply while you do the process. I'd like you to practice relaxing your body from the top of your head to the tips of your toes, one step at a time, until your body is completely and totally relaxed.

   b. Now, imagine yourself out in a beautiful, peaceful place, where you feel close to God. Give yourself a minute to enjoy the beauty of this place. Let your self drink in the beauty and feel that oneness with nature and with God. You may want to imagine yourself surrounded by angels who are there to help you and guide you in this process.

   c. Then find a comfortable place to sit down and relax in your peaceful place and as you sit, imagine a beautiful soft pink light coming down from above and pouring into your body through the top of your head and filling every cell of your body with a sparkling pink light. Soft pink is the color of Divine love. When the light has filled you, let it burst out and fill the entire area around you with this sparkling soft pink light of Divine love.

   d. Now imagine the people you love in front of you and imagine this Divine love flowing through you, down through the top of your head and out through your heart to each person that you love, one by one. As you fill and surround them with Divine love, imagine that they are radiant, healthy and happy. Don't try to figure out how they will change, just see the love filling and surrounding them and see them already happy and radiant. Let go and let God do the rest.

   e. Think of someone who you are having problems with in your life. Imagine them in front of you and send them Divine love as well. As you send them love, invite them to tell you what is going on in their life and what is hurting them. Ask them to tell you what you are doing that is making life more difficult for them and what you could do differently to make it better. Take this information into your heart and ask God to help you do your part to better this situation.

f. Before you come back, let the sparkling soft pink light of love fill you again and let yourself feel the natural joy and radiance it brings. Imagine your life getting better and better as you continue living your life from love and sending love to everyone you meet.

g. Now, slowly and easily, begin to bring your awareness back to your body. Take some big deep breaths and open your eyes. Take a few moments to ease yourself back into your normal waking consciousness.

h. Write your experience in your journal, so you'll be able to remember it later.

8. There are many wonderful books on living your spirituality. Go to a bookstore and look around if you're feeling a need for more input. Here are a few that have been helpful to me:
Return to Love, and *Illuminata,* by Marianne Williamson
Holy Spirit for Healing, by Ron Roth, Ph.D
Prayer is Good Medicine, by Larry Dossey, MD
Conversations with God, by Neale Donald Walsch
Divine Guidance, by Doreen Virtue, Ph.D.
Healing with the Angels, by Doreen Virtue Ph.D.
Anatomy of the Spirit, by Caroline Myss
Autobiography of a Yogi, by Paramahansa Yogananda
Compassion in Action, by Ram Dass and Mirabai Bush
The Power of Now, by Eckart Tolle
The Celestine Prophecy, by James Redfield
Messages From The Masters, by Brian Weiss MD
Awakening the Buddha Within, by Lama Surya Das
The Seat of the Soul, by Gary Zukav

9. If you would like obvious angelic guidance in your life on a daily basis, there are also some wonderful angel cards I'd recommend. They come with guidebooks for how to use them on a daily basis. Here are some of my favorites:

    Archangel Oracle Cards, by Doreen Virtue, Ph.D.

    Angel Blessings; Cards of Sacred Guidance and Inspiration, by Kimberly Marooney.

10. Write a few pages about how you are feeling after doing today's homework.

You are doing so wonderfully! I'm so proud of you! I want you to pat yourself on the back and acknowledge the time and effort you are putting into improving your life. You're going to be so happy when you see the changes that are coming. It will be worth every bit of effort you spent and far more!

Chapter Thirteen

Communicate With Love and Practice Win/Win Conflict Resolution!

Wes

Wes's early life was very tumultuous. He was born the fourth child of seven in a large Catholic family. His parents were loving to Wes but they fought regularly with each other. Wes's mother controlled the family except when his father got drunk and went into rage. Wes grew up terrified of his father's rage, but he was never allowed to express his feelings. His Mother had vowed to protect her children from all hurt and pain.

Wes started drinking with the men in his family when he was only seven years old. By the age of twelve, he was abusing alcohol regularly. At sixteen he dropped out of school and at seventeen he joined the army. After a year's training, Wes was sent to Viet Nam, where he rode helicopters and truck convoys, riding shotgun to protect the convoy.

In Viet Nam, Wes learned to be alert twenty-four hours a day. It was difficult to sleep because he never knew what to expect. Firefights were nothing compared to the utter helplessness and sheer terror of rockets coming out of the sky! Wes says he was brainwashed to believe that death and destruction were normal; that it was just another day.

Wes had grown up watching John Wayne movies where the honorable thing to do if your country went to war was to go defend your country. When he saw the real terror and destruction of the war, he felt very disillusioned and betrayed. He wondered if he'd ever make it home alive.

Wes came home on leave with shell shock and severe post-traumatic stress. He was ordered to go back after thirty days, but he refused. For four years he ran from the army, knowing they had the right in a time of war to shoot deserters if they found them. He was constantly on the move, supporting himself with small jobs or by dealing drugs. Eventually he was caught and sentenced to seven years in military penitentiary.

After serving his sentence for seven months, Wes got a presidential pardon. He went back on the road drinking and doing hard drugs until he got sick from 'agent orange.' For many years he went from one VA hospital to the next, trying to get help for his illness, but being refused because he didn't have an honorable discharge from the army. The last time he was refused medical help, he felt very angry when he saw a Vietnamese family in the hospital being taken care of by the medical staff.

Wes went to the medical staff and said, "I went to war for you and you kick me out of your hospital, but you take care of the Vietnamese people we were fighting against. I'm going home to fill my cowboy boots with dynamite and I'm coming back to blow up this hospital!" Wes was put in a psychiatric hospital and released to his parents after three weeks.

Wes's healing journey was long and difficult. With AA he was able to finally stop drinking, but when five family members including his mother died within two years, he had a relapse. After a six-day binge that made him so sick he couldn't see, he quit alcohol and hasn't ever touched it since.

Quitting alcohol was only the beginning. Owning his true

feelings was the hard part for Wes. It was painful and excruciating to face all the choices he had made and all the people he had hurt in the process. With the help of a loving wife and several counselors to guide the way, Wes was able to face the pain of his life. He learned how to communicate his feelings with love and respect and he made amends and started life anew.

Wes says he is still learning to forgive himself and love himself unconditionally. Today he is a very loving and respected man in his community. Many people now come to Wes for help and advice. In his job, he mentors young men from dysfunctional families and helps them to learn a trade and make a better life for themselves. After all that he's been through, Wes is truly an inspiration! If he can do it, so can you!

Days 25 and 26

So hello, again! How's your day going? Are you feeling happy and light-hearted? Have you been having any fun? Does it scare you to look at the topic we're discussing today? Communicating with love and practicing win/win conflict resolution is not something we learn in dysfunctional families, is it? Maybe it seems overwhelming to you right now, but don't worry! Before these two days are over you'll have a good handle on how to do exactly that. You'll be surprised and amazed to learn how simple it can be to bring love into your every day communication.

It's important that you realize that you are not alone. No one knows how to use healthy communication skills unless they've been taught or unless they've seen it role modeled in their families. Most of us learned all the wrong ways to communicate, not the right ways. Our dysfunctional families either didn't communicate feelings at all or they did it all wrong, by blaming, and attacking, and hating each other, and nothing ever being resolved. Does that sound familiar to you? I thought so.

I teach communication skills to people every day and I never run into anyone who learned how to communicate their feelings with love as a child. Remember what I told you back in Chapter One? The information for healthy communication simply wasn't available when we were young.

Even the most well meaning parents could only do the best they knew, and they simply didn't know the importance of talking about your feelings and learning how to resolve differences in a healthy way.

It's only since the 1990s that we have begun to realize the negative, long-term effects of verbal abuse. We didn't even know what verbal abuse was before that. I remember being miserable in a relationship I was in when I was young, but not understanding till years later what was wrong with that relationship. So relax! You're not stupid and you're not alone! Most people who come into my office to work on communication skills have created major problems in their relationships before they realize they need to do something different. In fact, one of my personal soapbox issues is that I strongly believe that healthy communication skills should be taught in our schools, so that people don't have to go through the pain of ruining their lives before they learn how to do it right.

So if you want to learn to communicate with love, you have to learn first of all to be patient, kind and gentle with yourself in this process. That includes all of you tough, macho guys! Even if it sounds wimpy to you, you absolutely have to learn how to be patient, kind and gentle with yourself or you'll never succeed.

Inside of every one of us is a hurting child, and that inner-child needs kindness and gentleness, not judgment and criticism, when we're learning new ways to communicate. Before you start this process, you have to recognize that you're not going to do it perfectly the first time. *The only way you'll learn to communicate with love is if you give yourself the right to make hundreds of mistakes, forgive yourself hundreds of times, and then start over, and try again every time!*

No matter how astute your mind is, when your emotions come into play you will go back to old patterns, and you'll think you're making a total fool of yourself if you still believe that you have to be perfect. The trick is to give up on having to be perfect and realize that learning is a process. Every time you go off track you simply learn how to bring yourself back on track. Emotional learning takes lots of time and patience.

Okay, then let's move on. The second step of learning to communicate with love is learning to be a good listener. You can't be a good communicator unless you can be sure that you have heard accurately what the other person is saying. Too often we don't really listen to what the other person is saying because we think we already know the other person's point of view, and we are too busy building our own case in the argument to really listen. If you want to communicate with love, you must learn to be a good listener.

One way to practice good listening skills is to paraphrase back to the other person what you heard them say in your own words, and then check with them to make sure you heard them accurately before you respond. Paraphrasing back what the other person said forces you to slow down and really listen before you talk, which helps the other person feel that you really care and that you actually heard what they said. Because you are changing your pattern of communicating, it also helps you program into your unconscious mind new, compassionate ways of communicating.

The third step in learning how to communicate with love is learning to respond rather than to react. 'Reacting' is when you get upset and fly off the handle at something someone did or said. When that happens, you usually say all the mean, hateful things that come to your mind, most of which you are sorry for later, but then it's forever too late to take them back. *Please remind yourself that many relationships have been damaged or destroyed by someone's ugly reactions.* As a therapist I get to see the consequences of those ugly reactions every day, and trust me, it's not pretty!

Responding, on the other hand, means instead of flying off the handle and losing your cool, you share your authentic feelings about what the other person said or did that bothered you. Instead of making them wrong and attacking them when you feel hurt or upset, you let them know what they did that hurt you or upset you. *I know it's scary to be vulnerable and share what hurt you after growing up in a family where no one cared about your feelings.* Believe me, I do understand. But you have to take the risk and learn a new way of communicating before you will see that it can be different now that you're an adult.

Learning to respond rather than to react simply takes a lot of time and effort. Reacting is just an ugly old habit that can be broken, but it takes consistent time and effort to do it a new way. This is where the quality of being kind and gentle with your self while learning your new communication skills becomes so crucial. Without that kindness and gentleness with your own inner child, you will probably lose patience and give up.

The fourth step in communicating with love is learning to use I-messages instead of you-messages. That means when you are upset, instead of saying "You dirty rotten bastard! You have totally ruined my life!" you say, "When you talk disrespectfully, I feel hurt and angry." I-messages are messages about you and your feelings. You-messages are opinions or judgments about the other person, and they usually come across as an attack.

When you use you-messages, you can expect that they will lead to the old dysfunctional way of doing conflict, which I call the 'attack-and-defend mode.' When you are using the old attack-and-defend conflict mode, nothing good will ever come from it! It always leads to hurt and ugliness. I-messages, on the other hand, create an opportunity for healing and resolution.

The old dysfunctional way of doing conflict in our marriages and families was the attack-and-defend, win/lose model. Someone won an argument and someone lost. In order for that to happen, each person was always trying to prove to the other that their way was the right way, and that if the other person would only agree, everything would be okay. The problem is, when you have two strong people in a relationship, you are never going to agree about all of your perceptions. Each person has their own perception of any given issue, based on their own history and background. You see, everybody sees the world through their own eyes, and when they look through their personal history and background, everybody is right.

Communicating with love involves using I-messages and talking from your heart to the people who matter most to you. That means you agree that it is okay to have different opinions or perceptions, but when you do, you will listen carefully and compassionately to each other's feelings. It's very important to try to understand how it feels to be in the other person's shoes.

When you both use I-messages and talk from your heart to each other and you have a deep understanding of each other's feelings, then you can begin to negotiate a win/win solution that works for everybody. You may never agree with your loved ones perceptions and opinions, but you can love and support them anyway, and you can still have a close, loving connection with them.

Communicating with love is so amazing when you actually experience it working! My clients are thrilled with the difference that it makes in their lives. It can turn a relationship around completely, from an angry, attacking relationship that just keeps getting worse, to a fun, lighthearted connection that gets better and better!

The last step of communicating with love is learning to use a simple little formula for expressing your feelings that I learned from a very inspiring man named Dr. Marshall Rosenburg. Dr. Rosenburg is inspiring to me because he works internationally in all kinds of amazingly difficult situations teaching both children and adults to meditate conflict using his simple little formula. The formula helps you to express your feelings clearly and precisely and then request the changes you'd like to see happen. It works beautifully, but the hard part is simply remembering to use it.

So, would you like to try it? Great! The formula has four phrases for you to complete, and it goes like this: "When you…I feel…because I need…and I'd appreciate…" All you have to do is fill in the blanks. For example: "When you come home late without calling first, I feel hurt and frustrated, because I need respect and understanding. I'd appreciate if you would call me when you know you're going to be late, so I can plan what I want to do accordingly."

Let me explain the phrases to you one at a time, so you understand how they work, okay? *"When you" is an observation totally free of judgment or evaluation.* What you want to do is just say what you see and hear as if you were looking through the lens of a camera, without any evaluation or opinion of what's going on. Remember in our example, we said "When you come home late without calling first…." but we did not say "You obviously don't care about me, because you just waltzed in the door two hours late like I don't matter!"

The second phrase is "I feel." *"I feel" is referring to your emotion, not your thoughts or images.* An example would be "I feel hurt or angry," but not "I feel that you are selfish and inconsiderate!" "I feel that" is not a feeling; it's a thought. Some examples of authentic feelings are sad, angry, hurt, frustrated, scared, happy, excited, or peaceful.

The third phrase is "because I need." *This is a universal need, which is a need that everyone shares.* An example would be "I feel hurt and frustrated, because I need respect," but not "I feel hurt because I need you to call me." Saying "I need you to" is not accurate. *If you think that you need someone else to change to make you happy, you will have big problems in your relationships. No one but you can be responsible to meet all your needs!* All you can do is communicate your universal needs clearly and then make a clear request that he or she do a specific action that meets a small part of your universal needs.

Universal needs are needs that we all share. They are the needs most anyone would have in the same situation. Some examples of universal needs you might have in different situations are respect, appreciation, understanding, compassion, integrity, acceptance, inclusion, consideration, equality, safety, clarity, trust, peace, connection, autonomy, cooperation, honesty, support, authenticity, play, challenge, meaning, purpose, and community.

The fourth phrase to the formula is "I'd appreciate." *"I'd appreciate" is leading to a specific do-able request, not a demand.* You can say "I'd really appreciate it if you'd call me as soon as you know you're going to be late," but don't say "I want you to call me immediately!" "I want you to" is a demand. It's very important that you remember to request rather than making a demand. When you communicate your feelings and your needs clearly and then make a specific, do-able request, people who love you will naturally want to help you and support you, but no one wants to do things that are demanded of them.

When you have communicated your feelings and your needs and requests clearly, then you simply need to step back and listen to the other person's response. Let them tell you what part of your request they are willing or not willing to do. Maybe you need to listen to their feelings again before you can go on and negotiate a win/win resolution to the issue at hand.

When you have both really listened compassionately to each other, and you both have a clear understanding of why the other person feels the way they do, then you can go on and brainstorm lots of possible win/win solutions to the problem, until you find one that works for both of you. Remember that there is no right answer. It's just finding the solution that feels good to both people involved.

So are you ready to do some homework? Relax! It's going to be fun! Just remember to be gentle and kind with yourself in this process, and keep your sense of humor. Everybody makes mistakes when they try to learn how communicate with love. Try to remember that perfection is not required. If you keep practicing over time, you will definitely improve your communication skills!

Homework Assignment: Chapter Thirteen

1.   First, I'd like you to write a paragraph about your own ability to be gentle and kind with yourself when you are learning something new. Are you interested in developing this quality for yourself?

2.   Now, I'd like you to write a paragraph about your own perception of your listening skills. Are you a good listener? Do you paraphrase back what you heard the other person say when there's a conflict? What could you do to improve your listening skills, based on the information you learned today?

3.   Write a paragraph about your personal experience with reacting rather than responding. Have you ever reacted when someone hurt you? What was the result of that communication? Did it get the results you hoped for? Has anyone you loved reacted rather than responded in his or her communication with you recently? How did that feel to you?

4.   How do you feel when someone uses you-messages when they are talking to you? Do you communicate your own feelings with I-messages rather than you-messages? Write about a recent experience of

both you-messages and I-messages, and how those experiences felt to you.

5. Okay, now think of a recent conflict you had with someone you love that did not turn out the way you wanted it to. Write a few paragraphs about what happened and about how you felt when it was over.

6. Think of the person you had the conflict with for a moment. I'd like you to write a paragraph about what he or she was feeling and why they were feeling the way they did, based on their history and their perception. Try to put yourself in their shoes and have compassion for how he or she must feel.

7. Now write a paragraph about what you were feeling in the conflict and why you felt this way, based on your history and your background. Be sure to separate your opinions or judgments from your feelings, because your opinions will not help you resolve the conflict.

8. Okay, I'd like you to put your feelings into the little formula we used by filling in the blanks. It goes "When you....I feel...because I need...and I'd appreciate....."

9. Write a paragraph about how you imagine the other person would have responded if you had communicated your feelings in this way.

10. Now brainstorm for a moment about what possible win/win solutions there could have been to this conflict that would have felt good to both of you. Write a paragraph or two about some of those win/win solutions.

11. Write a few pages in your journal about how you feel after doing today's homework.

12. If you want to learn more about the wrong ways and the right ways

of communicating, there are two books that I would recommend that could be very helpful to you. The first is about all the ways we communicate poorly. It's called *The Verbally Abusive Relationship*, written by Patricia Evans. The second book is about how to communicate with love. It's called *Non-Violent Communication*, written by Dr. Marshall Rosenberg.

Hey, great job! That was a challenging lesson, wasn't it? Don't expect yourself to communicate perfectly immediately. Just know that as you keep practicing the new way of communicating, it will eventually become a habit. When it does, it honestly becomes easy and fun!

Just be patient and kind with your self in the process of learning, okay? I'm very proud of you for your willingness to learn. Someday soon, you'll understand the importance of it all. You'll feel so much better when you see the results in your life that come from communicating with love!

Chapter Fourteen

Confront Your Greatest Fears and Pursue Your Passion!

Rikki

Rikki grew up in a traditional American family with two parents and an older brother. Her mom was kind and loving, but her dad was strict, authoritarian and verbally abusive. Rikki didn't have much fun as a child. Her dad put a lot of responsibility on her and expected a great deal. He also controlled the money in the family so much that Rikki only got one pair of shoes a year.

A friend of the family sexually abused Rikki when she was young, but she repressed the memory of abuse until she was older. She simply had no way to deal with her feelings at the time. Like other children from dysfunctional families, she never learned to express her feelings and needs as a child, and she grew up blaming herself and wondering what was wrong.

Rikki was twenty-eight years old when she first came to one of my personal growth workshops. She was a young stay-at-home mom at the time and had two small children. She was very committed to raising her family better than she had been raised, but she realized that in order to do that she had to heal herself.

Rikki told me many years later that she felt her life began when she came to that first workshop. She hadn't realized how unhappy she was until she began working through the feelings from childhood and releasing the emotional pain. She worked very hard to resolve her issues and when she started to feel better herself, she became very interested in helping others heal. Because she was so committed to her own personal growth, I invited her to become one of my workshop assistants. She told me later that she felt it was the highest compliment that she ever received.

New participants in the workshops often remarked about Rikki's kind, loving support when they were working through their issues. She could be very gentle and compassionate, yet at other times she was a real fireball, waking everyone up with her intensity and her humor. I could always count on Rikki to help people get to the bottom line. She never let the ball drop until she saw the smile of relief and lightheartedness on a participant's face.

The workshop community was very saddened when Rikki was diagnosed with bone cancer. We came together to support her and do everything we knew to help her heal, but we didn't have the tools necessary at the time to help her alter her destiny.

Rikki faced many fears in her life but I'm sure that none of them was as overwhelming as facing her fear of death. I was a weekly guest on a local television talk show the last few month's of Rikki's life. One day I asked Rikki if she'd be willing to write a few pages about her experience of facing her fear of death so that I could discuss it on the television show.

Rikki wrote an unbelievably beautiful essay entitled "Facing the Angel of Death." Her essay touched thousands of people's hearts that day when I shared it over the air. She started by saying "No one can die my death but me. There are so many people who love me and want to help me. I value and appreciate the energy they share with me, but when I face the angel of death, it is lonely. No one can walk those final steps but me.

"Every day is a precious gift. Thank you, God, that I woke up today! Sights and smells and sounds seem more intense. Colors are more vivid. The sky at dawn is beautiful but a different shade and quality than the beautiful blues and pinks of sunset. The blue of my children's eyes is too incredible to describe! Walking in the evening the smell of dew fills my lungs. Each breath cleanses and nourishes my hungry spirit. I must experience as many gifts from nature as possible while I'm still here.

"The taste of a breakfast peach is sweet and juicy. The bird-calls are brighter and more musical. My grandbaby's laughter is the most joyful and magical of sounds! The touch of my husband's arms and lips feels softer and stronger and more loving than ever before.

"I'm aware that angels are in constant contact and communication, even when I'm blocked or alone. Sometimes I see something; sometimes I hear; sometimes I just know. Their communication is non-verbal but I know I'm absorbing on another level. It's all good, and safe and completely non-threatening.

"Priorities become very clear. Sharing a precious day with friends and family is no contest over a television show. Beautiful music, laughter, fresh air, warmth and communion among friends far out-weighs being angry, temperamental, arrogant, critical, judgmental, or envious of others. It's more important now to give and receive love, show respect to others, listen to other's thoughts with open ears, and recognize each person's special gifts. The time to experience and experience life's wonders is a great priority!

"I am so incredibly thankful for every hug, every smile, every breath I can take! I am thankful for every loved one who calls and visits. I am thankful for every sparkle on the lake, very petal on the rose. I feel joy with every fiber and molecule of my being. Life is incredible, not to be wasted. Soak it up, store it up, and cherish every moment!

"I grieve with clarity. I cry daily. I know that I'm crying for a life cut short, for all the things I wanted to do, like planning my daughter's wedding, watching my son grow and become a father, or baking cookies for my grandson. I wish I could sail a boat again or ride a horse. I wish I could skip or dance, or jump, or even comb my own hair. Hope is like a ping-pong ball. One moment I know I'm healing and that I'll grow to be wise and elderly, and the next moment I feel like I will never be well.

"The angel of death is my friend. I know her well. We walk together, sit together, talk together and sleep together. I know it will be okay. She will take my hand as it slips from my husband's, and she will walk my next journey with me, and I will be safe!"

Days 27 and 28

So, how are you feeling today? Is this a good day for you? Are you feeling happy and lighthearted? If not, it really is okay! You will get there; it just takes time. If you're having a hard day, please remember that you can always go back to Chapter Three and work through any feelings or emotions that have come up. The process you did in Chapter Three is the basis for everything else in this book. You have to practice feeling and releasing your feelings regularly if you want the rest of this process to work for you.

You see, you've been working very hard on your personal growth through this process, and it's normal to get in touch with a lot of difficult old feelings in that process. If you haven't done this kind of emotional healing work before, your unconscious mind is full of memories and experiences that have never been resolved.

Remember that you need to be gentle and kind with yourself and take as much time as you need to heal those old unresolved feelings and experiences. It's like grieving the loss of your childhood in a sense, or the loss of a childhood you wish you could have had. Emotional healing takes time and effort, but when it's complete, you'll feel so much better!

So our topic today is confronting your fears and pursuing your passion. Maybe you're thinking, "I don't have fears! I'm a confident person!" Well, please read on, because I must say that I would beg to disagree with you. Fear can be very subtle and very much under the surface of our awareness.

Sometimes you don't even realize you have fear until you stop and think about where your life is now and where you would like it to be. If your life is not everything you want it to be right now, you do have fears that you aren't addressing whether you realize it or not. Often we get so accustomed to our little comfort zones, that we really don't want to face what it takes to get out of them. It's much easier to sit and complain about how bad it is than to do the work it takes to face our fears and move forward in our lives.

I think a good definition of fear is that *fear is the feelings from the past projected on the future.* Most of us have had experiences at some point in our lives when we tried to do something that didn't work and because it was painful to us in some way, we simply didn't try anymore. Our fear, in this case, is that the same thing could happen again. I think you know how that feels, don't you?

Let's try an example, okay? Maybe you really would love to have a good friend to talk to on a daily basis, but sometime in your life, someone whom you trusted as a friend really hurt you in some way. Maybe now you don't try any more because you don't ever want to get hurt like that again. So, you see, it's your fear of being hurt again that keeps you from reaching out and making new friends today.

Or maybe you're working a job that you hate, but at some point in your life you tried finding something better, and for some reason it just didn't work out so now you simply don't try anymore. Does this sound familiar? *Fear is always what keeps us from moving forward in our lives to make our lives better than they are today.* If we had no fear, we'd be happy, fulfilled human beings, having warm, loving families and great support systems, and doing work that we love every day and being paid what we really deserve for our efforts. Doesn't that sound like fun?

So today we're going to work on overcoming your fear. Are you ready? Okay, I want you to start thinking about something you would really love to see change in your life, but somewhere deep inside you're feeling afraid to do what it takes to make this change. Can you think of something like that in your life? Are you afraid to have close friends because you'd have to let people see who you really are? Are you afraid they would judge you or laugh at your feelings? Are you afraid to go back to school to better your career, because you're too old and you're sure the younger students would out-do you and make you feel stupid?

Are you afraid to change jobs or start a business that you know you would love, because you might lose your financial security and not be able to support your family? Yes, that's a good one, isn't it? We're all afraid of losing our financial security. Well, relax, because I'm not going to suggest that you quit your job tomorrow and open a new business. I would never suggest that you borrow money and lose everything you have so you end up being a homeless person or a bag lady! I just want you to think about where you are today, and where you'd like to be, and then take baby steps in that direction every day until you get there. Is that fair?

If you really want to make changes in your career, and you know that it requires more schooling, then call around and start asking questions. You could also look on the internet and find what is available and just start corresponding with people who can help you. Maybe you're saying, "I just don't have the money. I'd really love to do what you're asking, but I'm so financially strapped, there's just no way." I just don't buy that excuse, sorry! I've heard it a thousand times and I still don't buy it. I know from lots of experience with myself and with others, that the old saying really is true; where there's a will there's a way!

You see, it's not the money; it's your fear that is stopping you. Money just gives you an acceptable excuse that other people relate to and then you can continue commiserating with them about how miserable your life is. Is that the way you want to live, with fear running your life?

Maybe your fear has you so locked up inside that you can't even think of what you could do to make your life better. If that's true for you, just start brainstorming with people you know and ask them for ideas they might have that could help you. Or you could start imagining your life changing in a positive direction, even though you don't know what the direction is.

You can always ask God and your angels to help you and show you what you can do. That plan always works if you just keep asking till you get the answers. Just be sure that while you're praying you also ask for willingness to face the truth! Whatever you do, just don't give up and let your fear continue to control your life. It's when you give up that the ball stops rolling. As long as you are making an effort to confront your fears in some small way, then your life will continue changing in a positive direction.

If you're feeling really stuck and you really don't know what to do, you could also try professional help. Don't be afraid to go to a mental health professional if you feel the need. Thank God that in this new century seeking professional help is no longer something to be ashamed of. It's just another way to get through those challenges you are facing. Who knows, you may meet someone wonderful who can really help you change your life for the better!

Remember that if you do reach out for professional help and you're not getting the help you need, you don't need to be afraid to move on and keep looking till you find someone who is right for you. You don't have to stay with the first professional you find. It's always okay to get a second opinion.

So now that you're ready to confront those fears that you have, let's get on to the real fun today. Let's think about pursuing your passion! Pursuing your passion is about finding what excites you in life and creating a way to bring that into your life in some way on a regular basis. The ideal, of course, would be to do what you really love as your career, and immerse yourself in it every day of your life. Doesn't that sound like fun? Of course, if that's not possible for you to do immediately, you can always start with doing what you love as a hobby, and then letting it grow and build until you find a way to earn your living doing it.

I know that growing up in a dysfunctional family sometimes damages you so much that you don't even know what you love. You struggle so much with daily survival that you don't have time to think about what you want or what you enjoy. If you're feeling this way right now, you can always go back to Chapter Ten and spend more time getting to know yourself and paying attention to what you enjoy on a day-to-day basis. Remember, it's okay to take as much time as you need.

There's no rush here, and no one to answer to but yourself. Just keep writing in your journal on a regular basis about what you enjoy until you find something that really excites you. As you keep working through your old feelings and releasing them like we did in Chapter Three, it gets much easier to know what excites you. Trust me, you will get there! It's just a process of following those little clues your awareness gives you until they start to come together and create a picture of what you really love.

Shirley Luthman, the author of *Energy and Personal Power*, wrote years ago that the way to pursue your passion to "go where the juice is!" That's a great phrase to remember! If you "go where the juice is," you will follow what excites you, and fascinates you and what gives you joy. What could be more fun than that?

If you've always wanted to learn yoga, why not go take a class in it? Who knows, maybe you'll go on some day to become a yoga teacher after taking that first class like one of my clients did. If you've always wanted to study architecture, go sign up for a class! Or if you always wanted to be a teacher, think about what you have learned in your life that you might be able to teach. Who knows, maybe you could fulfill your desire to teach in a different way.

Or maybe it's time to go back to school and get your teaching degree. It's never too late, you know! My mother went to college when she was fifty even though she had never gone to high school. After raising ten children, she went back to college and became a special education teacher. She fulfilled her life-long dream and she had a very happy ten years as a teacher before she retired.

One of my clients who always loved babies now works as a 'dula' helping new mothers care for their babies, and she loves it! She also teaches infant massage on the side. Another of my clients went through a painful divorce and was fascinated with the mediation process, so he took some classes and became a mediator. Another client was hurt in an accident and had to change careers. She worried and fretted for a time and then in the process of going to physical therapy, she decided she wanted to be a physical therapist. She is now absolutely thrilled with her new career!

You may remember me saying that I became a counselor in my early twenties because I was depressed myself when I was young. When I got better, I became fascinated with helping others who were in emotional pain and then I went on to become a psychotherapist. So, you see, if you pay attention, life itself has a way of taking you where you need to go.

There's an incredible quote about overcoming our fear and shining our light in the world that I'd like to share with you today before we complete. It's from Marianne Williamson, the author of *Illuminata*. Nelson Mandela quoted this in his inaugural speech in South Africa. It goes like this: "Our deepest fear is not that we are inadequate, our deepest fear is that we are powerful beyond measure. It is our light, not our darkness, that most frightens us. We ask ourselves, who am I to be brilliant, gorgeous, talented and fabulous? Who are you not to be? You are a child of God. Your playing small does not serve the world. There is nothing enlightened about shrinking so that other people won't feel insecure around you. We were born to make manifest the glory of God that is within us. It's not just in some of us; it is in everyone. As we let our own light shine, we unconsciously give other people permission to do the same. As we are liberated from our own fear, our presence automatically liberates others." Isn't that an incredibly beautiful thought?

So to wrap it up for today, confronting your fears and pursuing your passion can be a bit of a challenge at times, but it's so worthwhile in the long run! When you overcome those life-long fears, and find your passion, and spend your time doing what you love, your life can change so dramatically that you almost don't recognize it. It's very exciting! Little by little, you start to see changes that you never would have believed possible. When you get to the point of really living what you feel passionate about, you will honestly feel like you're living in heaven. It's truly incredible!

So let's get to work. Pull out your journal and let's get busy, okay?

Homework Assignment: Chapter Fourteen

1. Think about something you really want in your life, but you're just too afraid to act on. Write a paragraph about it, and about why it's so scary to you.

2. Now write a paragraph about what your life would be like if you were able to get past your fear and do whatever it takes to bring this wonderful new addition into your life.

3. Now brainstorm some ideas of things you could do to move a baby step in the direction of facing your fears. Write a few paragraphs about your ideas.

4. Now I'd like you to write a paragraph about something that really excites you that you would love to know more about. Write about how you could learn more about this topic or how you could bring it into your life in some way.

5. Okay, now I'd like you to think about what your life would be like if you could, by some miracle, do what you love as a career. How would it benefit you if you were able to achieve this dream? How would it feel? I'd like you to hang out in the feeling of living your dream for as long as you can today and then write a few paragraphs about that feeling.

    Remember the power of imagination is to imagine your dream already here, and enjoy the incredible feeling of living it and breathing it right now. If you really want to manifest this dream into reality, come back and imagine it again for five minutes every day until it manifests beautifully and magnificently in your life.

6. If you want to learn more about overcoming your fears, there are several great books you can read:
    Feel the Fear and Do It Anyway, by Dr. Susan Jeffers
    The Success Principles, by Jack Canfield

The Best Year of Your Life: Dream It, Plan It, Live It by Debbie Ford.

7. If you want to develop your own creative gifts and find a way to earn a living doing what you love, there are also many books available. There's one great book that I'd recommend that's called *The Artist's Way*, by Julia Cameron. Julia Cameron gives you a twelve-week process for pursuing your creativity that's very fun to follow. You don't have to be a painter or a musician or a writer to be an artist. It's a wonderful book to read for anything creative you want to do in your life.

8. Write a few pages about how you feel after doing today's homework.

Wow! You're doing so wonderful! You're going to be so much happier with your life when you start facing your fears and moving through them. Your world is changing, and you're going to be thrilled when you see the results. Keep up the good work!

Chapter Fifteen

Infuse Your Life With Love, Harmony and Beauty!

Princess Diana

Diana was the third child in a family of four. When she was six years old, her parent's divorced and she and her brother and two older sisters lived with her father. The two older sisters were sent off to boarding school, but Diana and her brother were raised by numerous nannies. When they went to visit her mother on weekends, Diana remembers seeing her mother crying every Saturday night because she didn't want them to go home.

Diana said her childhood was unhappy and very unstable. She always felt detached and very different from everyone else. She said she felt like she was a nuisance to have around, because she knew her parents wanted a boy when she was born. At times she felt hopeless, like she wasn't good at anything, compared to her brother who was far more successful in school.

From a young age Diana felt she had an important mission to fulfill in life. When she was just thirteen she told her father that she felt she was going to marry someone in the public eye. Yet, at sixteen when Prince Charles first showed an interest in her, she was amazed that he would be interested in her. When he asked her to marry him at eighteen, she said, "Yes, please," because she didn't know what to say or do.

Diana became bulimic before the wedding happened, because of a remark Charles made about her chubby waist. She wanted so much to please him that she went from a 29-inch waist to 23 inches in only a few months. The night before her wedding she had a bout of bulimia, but on her wedding day she was calm. She said she felt like she was a lamb being led to the slaughter.

It soon became obvious to Diana that Charles was in love with his former lover Camilla. Diana overheard Charles on the telephone during that time saying to Camilla, "Whatever happens, I will always love you." He also had a special bracelet made for Camilla that he gave to her two days before his wedding to Diana.

We've all heard the rest of the story. Diana was a princess trapped in a castle. She had very little love and support from the royal family. She was very sad and depressed and sometimes even suicidal, but she tried, overall, to make the best of a bad situation. She gave birth to two beautiful sons and dedicated herself to raising them differently than the rest of the royal family. In time Diana ventured out and began to make a difference in the world.

I never met Diana, but it's obvious to me that she took her own emotional healing journey. She found love and support wherever she could from her friends and her royal staff. She also found therapists and teachers to help her along the way. It's only someone who has overcome tremendous emotional pain that can give the heart-felt, sincere caring that Diana was able to give.

We remember Diana for her beauty, her laughter, and her heart. Everywhere she went in the last years of her life, she demonstrated her unique, indescribable beauty, both inside and out. She cared for people who were dying of aids and terminal illnesses, and she held babies in her arms who had been traumatized by landmines. She worked tirelessly for charity, and was loved by the public for her warmth and humanity.

Princess Diana's sudden death led to an unprecedented worldwide outpouring of grief and love. As her brother said at her funeral, she was "the unique, the complex, the extraordinary and irreplaceable Diana, whose beauty, both internal and external, will never be extinguished from our minds." People who were near Diana said she dearly wanted to help people learn to share their emotions more fully. Sadly, in her untimely death, that goal was accomplished with people crying all over the world.

After she died, Margaret Thatcher, the former prime minister of Great Britain said, "With the tragic death of Princess Diana, a beacon of light has been extinguished. Her good works brought hope to so many of those in need throughout the world."

Princess Diana, wherever you are, we love you!

Days 29 and 30

Hello there! How are you today? Isn't life getting to be fun and interesting? It's a beautiful day today! Don't you think so? Actually it's a beautiful day every day when you decide to make it beautiful. Hey, that's what we get to talk about today, love, harmony and beauty! I'm looking forward to this lesson. I hope you are too. What could be more fun than love, harmony and beauty?

I was thinking about you this morning while I was sitting and meditating in my living room in front of a little altar I've created. I was asking myself how I could show you how to create a life of love, harmony and beauty? I actually talked to my angels about it because they often have good ideas. Sometimes my angels can be quite funny. It's like they're saying "Don't you get it? The answer is right in front of you!"

So, of course, the suggestion they were trying to give me was to invite you to try some of the things I've tried in my life, because they've always worked for me. You see, long ago, I felt just as scared and alone as you may think you are right now. I learned it all the long, hard way, but lucky you, you've got this fun, little book to help you get there more quickly!

So let's get started! I think it's important to realize that love, harmony, and beauty are all qualities of the Divine. Whether you call it God, or your Higher Power or whatever you feel comfortable with, if you want to bring these qualities into your everyday life, a good place to start is to talk to your Higher Power and ask for help and guidance.

One way to do that is to create an altar in your home, where you go whenever you can to spend time with God. If you want to create an altar that's meaningful and personal to you, just think about what reminds you of God and then gather little symbols of God to place on your altar. Those symbols help you tune in to your Higher Power whenever you want to meditate or pray. For example, I've got candles, and angels, and a beautiful bouquet of fresh flowers, as well as a picture of the Ascended Christ on my altar because that's what reminds me of God, but you could put whatever feels Divine or holy to you.

Praying and meditating doesn't have to be done at any special time of day or in any particular way. I love praying and meditating first thing in the morning because I think it starts my day off better, but you could actually do it any time of day. God doesn't care what time you choose. It's totally up to you! There are also thousands of ways to pray and meditate and thousands of people out there who will tell you their way is the right way and the only way, but I'll tell you my secret about that. *There is no right way to pray and meditate! Just do it!*

I like to sit comfortably in front of my altar with my spine fairly straight because that creates a clear energy channel in my body. Then I invite God and the angels to be with me. I just tell them about my concerns for whatever is going on in my life and then I ask for help and guidance in overcoming any challenges I might have. I've learned that when I'm asking for the good of everyone, not just myself, and I have a sincere, pure heart about it, I can actually feel the energy of the angels coming in to help me. Sometimes it makes me very high and blissful. It's like actually feeling a higher level of consciousness. Try it! It's very fun!

Calling on your angels is really pretty simple. Remember that there are thousands of unemployed angels out there just waiting for our invitation for them to help us with our lives. They can't interfere with our life unless we invite them unless we're in a life-threatening situation. But when we do invite them, they can be a big help in our lives as well as a lot of fun. Give it a try and you'll see for yourself.

Some people actually see angels and I think that would be wonderful, but you don't have to see them to know that they are real. When you invite your angels to help you, you may hear words or messages in your mind, or you may have ideas come to you out of the blue, or you may find that you just know things from deep inside yourself even though you don't know how you know them. The angels communicate in many different ways. When you ask for their help, just be sure to pay close attention to any intuition or inner guidance that comes, because you'll always get it if you're paying attention.

Doreen Virtue, in her book *Divine Guidance,* has some wonderful insight on how to differentiate true divine guidance from our ego's false guidance. She says the ego's false guidance is always based on fear. It tears down your confidence, weakens you, and drains your energy and enthusiasm.

True, divine guidance, on the other hand, has a loving, energizing feeling to it. It empowers you; it sounds supportive and motivational; and it often talks about your life's purpose or your mission in the world. Divine guidance will often come suddenly. It may feel like it's "out of the blue," but it will often be in response to your prayers.

Listening to your own intuition or guidance helps you start to actually feel connected to the Divine. It's a great feeling to know that there is someone out there helping you and guiding you to make your life better. It makes you feel like you do matter, even when the world outside might be giving you other messages.

When you're asking for Divine help for creating more love, harmony and beauty in your life, your angels will definitely guide you. What I'm going to share with you today are some of the ways that have worked for me in the past, just to give you some ideas or possibilities.

To me it's very important to feel human love and support on a daily basis, so one of the first things I asked for years ago before I had a family of my own was one true friend. I started by imagining or visualizing having a real, true friend, and then I followed my intuition about which friendships to pursue. I had to go through trying several friendships that didn't feel quite right before I finally found one that I knew I could really count on. My one true friend and I got through years of pain and suffering by sharing our tears and laughter with each other on a regular basis. I know now that having one real friend to cry and laugh with on your emotional healing journey is truly a gift from God.

Having that one true friend helped me create a loving family as I grew and matured. When you know the feeling of receiving unconditional love, it becomes much easier to give it to the important people in your life. To me it was very healing and fulfilling to love my children unconditionally. By loving them unconditionally, it also helped to heal the child within me. I got a tremendous joy when my children were young by simply letting them be children and watching them play unrestrictedly. Watching their spontaneous joy and happiness often helped me heal the emotional pain of my own life.

Another way I found pure, unconditional love through the years was having pets in my home that loved me unconditionally. I learned very young that my cats were always happy to see me, no matter what was going on in my life. I found a t-shirt once that said, "Cats are angels with fur," and I think sometimes it's really true. When things are difficult in our lives, angels can help us feel divine, unconditional love through our pets. Having a pet that loves us unconditionally can often help to bring us out of grief or depression by making us smile and laugh again. Even research has shown that loving a pet can lift a person's spirit out of depression and grief.

So shall we move on? Let's talk about bringing harmony into your life. One way that harmony comes to us is in the form of beautiful music. Music, to me, is an incredible gift from God. It makes me feel alive and connected to the Divine. There are obviously lots of ways to enjoy music in your life. You can simply play it on your stereo, or you can sing and dance in your home, or you can actually learn to play a musical instrument yourself.

So many times in my life when I was down and out, my intuition would bring beautiful music to me in some way. Often in those difficult times, it was music that would lift my spirits and give me hope again. I'm sure you know what I mean. Harmonious music can be very healing and so very refreshing!

Of course it's also very important to create harmony in our families. Often a feeling of love and harmony in our families starts by simply acknowledging the good in each other on a regular basis. Simply giving each member of your family a sincere compliment every day can make a huge difference. Too often we focus on what's wrong in each other instead of on what's right and good and what we really value and appreciate in each other. Focusing on what you like about each other creates a bond of love and appreciation between you.

Another way to bring a feeling of love and harmony into your family is to really listen and care about each other's feelings and needs. Instead of getting angry and defensive when someone needs your love and support, try breathing deeply and really listening to what they are saying. Taking time to really listen to each other and care about each other's feelings and needs makes your relationships feel completely new and different. You can also support each other's goals, dreams and successes if you want to help each member of your family feel truly loved and supported.

You can also bring harmony into your life through creating a support system of friends who love you dearly and really want the best for you. When you have a group of loving, supportive friends, you can all get together to celebrate the important occasions of life, like birthdays, holidays, graduations, weddings or funerals, or whatever feels important to you.

I have a pillow in my counseling office that someone gave me that says, "Friends become our chosen family." That's so very true. Even if you came from a very dysfunctional family that doesn't want to change, you can always create a loving, supportive family of friends. Often you'll find that holidays and celebrations are more fun with your new family than they were with the old one.

Maybe you're saying, "Wait up here! I'm still looking for that one true friend. How am I supposed to find a whole group of them?" I know.

It's that 'patience and persistence over time' thing again. You start with one friend, and then you find another, and over time, you create a loving support system for yourself.

One of the easiest ways to make true, wonderful friends is to be the unexpected angel in other people's lives. When you see someone who is having a hard day or going through difficult time in his or her life, think of something you could do to brighten his or her day. What could you do to make that person's life easier in some way?

When you take the time to think of his or her feelings and find a way to make their his or her life better, often he or she will want to do the same for you when the tables are turned. It's a very fun, magical experience when it happens. Over time, that person could become one of your dearest life-long friends. I know it's true, because most of my dearest friendships started in that way.

Okay, shall we talk about creating beauty in your life? Beauty became important to me when I began to get emotionally healthy. I noticed then that beauty made me feel closer to the Divine. My problem was, back in the old days, that I didn't have much money to create beauty around myself. I was doing good to be able to afford the bare essentials in life at that time.

Early on I learned that I could always go out in nature and feel the beauty of nature around me. I learned to drink the beauty of nature into my soul and take it with me wherever I went. I noticed that I always felt better when I spent time out in nature.

I also learned that I could find beautiful things to bring into my life in all kinds of interesting, creative ways. By following my guidance and intuition, I found lots of ways to create beauty in my life even while I was on a very limited budget. One way of bringing beauty into my home was just to have a bouquet of fresh flowers on the table whenever I could. Sometimes I picked them myself and sometimes I'd bring them home from the supermarket. Fresh flowers have such a wonderful way of bringing the indescribable beauty of nature right into your home.

Another way I learned to create beauty in my life was by choosing clothes to wear that made me feel special and beautiful inside and out. I noticed that when I wore attractive clothes, I felt better about myself. I loved dressing my little girls in pretty clothes that showed their beauty and charm. Sometimes the clothes we found were hand-me-downs, but with keeping an eye for beauty, we could still make them look pretty and fun. Through following my guidance, I became an expert at shopping the department store sales at the end of the season and finding beautiful things at very low prices.

When I continued my quest for beauty, I also found all kinds of inexpensive ways to redecorate our home, like finding wallpaper on a closeout sale to redecorate a room or finding furniture and home accessories at garage sales. It became a fun, creative project to find the best deals for almost nothing and still create a sense of beauty and grace in our environment. With patience and persistence, we were able to create a home that felt bright and energetic.

Over the years I continued to visualize and ask for Divine help in creating a more beautiful home environment. After a number of years, even though I was still a single Mom with two daughters to raise and educate, I was able to build a beautiful home on a mountaintop overlooking a gorgeous lake. Yes, I'm aware that it was a miracle, but it was a miracle that I visualized regularly in advance, and I kept asking for divine help and guidance and I simply didn't give up until I got there.

Don't tell me that you can't create miracles because I know you can. Remember what I've said about patience and persistence over time? You just have to take your natural stubbornness and turn it into persistence and you'll be well on the way to success!

I remember very clearly what it took to bring about the miracles in my life. I had the same tools I've given you in this book, so I know that you can do it too. If you visualize what you want regularly, and ask your angels for help and guidance, and then do everything you know to bring it about, it does happen in time. It's so much fun to see how it comes! Try it for yourself and just don't ever give up until you get there.

You may be thinking that I make it all sound too easy. I've heard that before. But don't give up before you try. Remember I didn't say it would be easy. Keeping yourself focused positively on making your life better is not at all easy. You'll probably fall down a thousand times in the process and have to pick yourself back up over and over, just like I did. But if you train yourself to always come back to your positive focus, even when you go off track temporarily, you're going to get there over time.

So, do you want to do some homework today? I think you're going to enjoy it. We're getting to the good stuff now, don't you think?

Homework Assignment: Chapter Fifteen

1. Create an altar somewhere in your house, where you can go to pray and meditate. Look around your house or go out in nature and collect things that remind you of God and then place them on your altar. I'd love it if you'd be willing to write about your experience of creating an altar. I think you'll enjoy reading that someday down the road.

2. Find time in your day to pray and meditate when you can. Doing it daily would be wonderful, but if you can't manage that right now, start with whatever you can fit into your life.

3. There are many wonderful books on meditating and receiving divine help and guidance. Some that I've enjoyed are listed here:
    Wherever You Go, There You Are; Mindfulness Meditation in Everyday Life, by Jon Kabat-Zinn
    Illuminata, by Marianne Williamson
    Reclaim Your Spiritual Power, by Ron Roth, Ph.D.
    Divine Guidance, by Doreen Virtue, Ph.D
    Healing With The Angels, by Doreen Virtue
    Archangels and Ascended Masters, by Doreen Virtue, Ph.D.
    An Angel's Guide to Heaven on Earth, by Susan Ann Gossett
    Ask Your Angels, by Alma Daniels, Timothy Wiley and Andrew Ramer

4. Ask God and your angels for help and guidance about how you can bring more love, harmony and beauty into your life and write a few paragraphs on the thoughts and ideas that come to you.

5. What can you do today and tomorrow to take action on some of the

ideas that you've received? Write a paragraph about how you can start today with infusing your life with love, harmony and beauty.

6. If you would like obvious angelic guidance in your life on a daily basis, remember the angel cards that I've recommended before. They come with guidebooks for how to use them on a daily basis. In case you've forgotten, here are a couple of my favorites:
Archangel Oracle Cards, by Doreen Virtue, Ph.D.
Angel Blessings; Cards of Sacred Guidance and Inspiration, by Kimberly Marooney.

7. Write a paragraph on you could be the unexpected angel in someone else's life this week. What could you do to brighten his or her day, or to make his or her life easier? Remember that when you take the time to give from your heart to others, often they will want to give back to you. Even if it doesn't come back from them personally, it will always come back to you in other ways.

8. How can you keep yourself focused on creating more love, harmony and beauty in your life over time, even when you get off track at times? I'd like you to write about ways you know to develop patience and persistence over time.

9. Write a few pages about how you feel after doing today's homework.

Wow! I'm so proud of you! You're really making progress! I want you to pat yourself on the back today and tell yourself what a great job you're doing. Your life will never be the same. You're going to be so happy that you took this journey! Keep up the good work! We're definitely getting somewhere now.

Chapter Sixteen

Develop Your Sense of Humor and Laugh Till You Wet Your Pants!

Kathy

Kathy was the elder of two daughters in a traditional religious family. Her family was very oriented to following the rules of society. Both parents had very high ideals and wanted very much to be perfect. Kathy tried hard as a child to please them, to be a good girl, and to act appropriately so that no one would think badly of her family.

In many ways, Kathy's childhood was ideal, so she could never understand why she always felt so bad about herself inside. She says her parents were extremely upset by anything that was different from them because they simply couldn't fathom any differences. They always tried to do what was right in their own minds for Kathy, but they never allowed her to be her real self. For example, they told Kathy regularly that her feelings were not real. If she said, "I feel sad," they would say "Why do you feel sad?" then "No, you don't really feel sad!"

Kathy lived her early life almost entirely in her mind and her thoughts. She actually had to be taught what a gut feeling was when she got into therapy at twenty-two years old. When she learned to live from her own feelings, she began to tell the whole truth all the time. She wanted her life would be her own instead of living just to get the approval of others.

Kathy says she was thrilled by the changes she could see as a result of emotional healing, but she was horrified by her own lack of emotional maturity. She says it was extremely painful to her to be so emotionally immature. After Kathy began healing her emotions, she became more alive and more joyful.

Gradually Kathy went from having only one good day a week to having only one bad day. Her time lag for recognizing her own anger went from four years to only four hours. Kathy describes the process of emotional healing as a gradual freedom that came a little bit at a time from the constant emotional pain. Telling the truth, getting free of the emotional backlog, and feeling love in her heart all wove together to give her the self empowerment and sense of connection to the world that she had always hoped for.

Kathy and I met in our early twenties. We were young, inexperienced therapists back then running emotional therapy groups. Our friendship bonded and deepened over the years as we learned and grew together, always supporting each other's emotional healing process in the best way we knew. Kathy was my one true friend that got me through unbelievable pain in my life so many times when there was no one else to count on! She taught me, by her example, what unconditional love is all about.

Laughter has always been an important part of our friendship. Laughing at the ridiculousness of our dramas becomes funny after we find our way through the pain. We've often found that even our most insurmountable issues can become hilarious when seen through a new and different perspective. Although no one else's emotional pain is ever funny when they're feeling it, the way we trap our selves and share the same dilemmas in our healing process makes wonderful material for humor.

Today Kathy is happily married to a wonderful man. She has a loving support system of friends who face their issues and choose to heal emotionally and spiritually. She is very committed spiritually and over the years spirituality has become a primary focus in her life. Kathy still laughs regularly and she very much enjoys the funny side of personal growth and spirituality.

Kathy is also a phenomenal psychotherapist. She loves the exciting work she is now able to do with her clients. Kathy was able to take the emotional pain of her early life and transmute it into a pristine knowledge and awareness that now supports her clients to totally transform their lives!

Days 31 and 32

Hi there! How are you today? I'm so glad to see that you hung in there with me through an entire month of your life! Life is very precious you see, and your willingness to take these thirty-three days out of your life to focus on your personal growth is undoubtedly going to change your life forever. It will make you appreciate life and all it has to offer, and it will definitely help you have more fun and live more lightheartedly.

In fact I'd venture a guess that if you've made it this far, you are probably already having fun and feeling more lighthearted. It's pretty hard to do all the work you've been doing and not feel the natural, lighthearted affects that come from it.

But if you're not feeling lighthearted today, relax! Don't worry! I didn't start out being a lighthearted person. Years ago people used to ask me why I never smiled and why I was so serious all the time. When you have years of unresolved issues all balled up inside you with no way to release them, you don't feel much like smiling. So, if you're feeling sad, or hurt, or frustrated today, just go back and do the feelings homework on Chapter Three one more time before you go on with today's lesson.

You may also need to review the forgiveness process in Chapter Seven to make sure you have forgiven everyone, including yourself. You'll never get to lightheartedness while you're still blaming yourself or someone else for your problems, or expecting someone else to make you happy. But don't worry; you have a lifetime of lightheartedness ahead of you, so one more day is no big deal! If you simply remain persistent about it, you are going to get there. It's just a matter of time!

Drunvelo Melchizedek in the Spirit of Ma'at online webzine said that the ancient Egyptians had a tradition that said that 'Lightness of Heart' was crucial to a spirit's ability to transcend into the higher worlds. They taught that if your heart was lighter than a feather at the time of your death, then your soul could proceed on to the higher realms. If not, then your soul would have to reincarnate on the earth, hoping next time to live a life that would bring this all-important Lightness of Heart. I loved hearing that because I've always had a strong feeling about the value of joy and lightheartedness.

You see, our true spirit is made up of joy, freedom and bliss, but it's only when we can reconnect to that true spirit that we feel that blissfulness. Releasing our dysfunctional family issues helps us to free ourselves of our emotional baggage and to reconnect with the essence of our true spirit.

So you're probably wondering how to get there from here. Remember the old joke where someone was asking directions and the answer was "You can't get there from here!" Well, relax; I know you can get there from here! You absolutely can become a lighthearted person if you want to, and trust me, the time and energy it will take is well worth your effort. Life is so much more interesting and fun when you live your life lightheartedly.

The way I started years ago was by imagining or visualizing myself laughing and having fun. I actually visualized laughing like I did when I was a child, till I rolled on the floor laughing. I imagined laughing until I literally wet my pants. I'll admit I had to stretch my mind to believe that it could really happen at the start, but I also remember the incredible feeling when it did start to happen. I was practicing music with some friends of mine one evening, and something struck us as funny, and we all laughed so hard we literally rolled on the floor. Laughing like that was so unbelievably freeing. It was like taking twenty years of baggage off our shoulders and feeling like kids again.

For the past twenty years, I've given weekend personal growth workshops a couple times a year to give people a safe place to heal their dysfunctional family issues. Those workshops have literally been the highlight of many people's lives, because when people release their emotional issues and reconnect with their true selves, everyone starts to be silly and just have fun.

No one is worried anymore about impressing others in that environment and no one is wondering about what other people are thinking of them. They're just happy being themselves. When you find that kind of inner peace and happiness, the playful child in you comes out naturally and he or she just wants to play and have fun. At that point, we don't need alcohol or drugs to be able to have fun, because we are literally high on life!

So, that's where we want to go, you and I, to that natural lightheartedness that comes from releasing the old baggage and just being high on life. Don't worry; I'm not suggesting that you go back to denying your emotional pain. Denial is not the answer! Denial never works long-term; it's only a temporary fix.

When you think you've got your denial well in place and you think you're absolutely in control, God just laughs and finds another way to turn your life upside down till you really get the point. You see, God knows that's what we're really here for. *We're here to remember that we are actually spiritual beings having a human experience.* We're here to learn how to create heaven on earth and how to live from love, joy, peace, and lightheartedness every day!

Are you wondering how you can develop that natural lightheartedness if you've gotten out of the habit? Good question! Changing your old habits might be exactly the place to start. I'd suggest that you start by doing something different that gets you out of the rut you've been in for the last five or ten years. Go to new places, read new books, talk to new people. Plan a new activity that you've never done before once a week, or even once a month. Just having a change of scenery and some new interesting people in your life can help you start to make the changes you want to make.

Then you could try doing what I did. Imagine laughing like you did when you were a youngster, just being silly, and carefree, and not having a worry or a care in the world. I'd suggest you hold this image of you laughing like you did as a child in your mind every day for at least five minutes, and really have fun imagining it, until you start to see the changes in your life.

You can also find people in your life who like to laugh and spend time with them. You can learn a lot from people who have developed their own sense of humor. If you hang out with people who like to laugh on a regular basis, their ability to see the funny side of life will soon wear off on you. You'll find your own natural wit and humor starting to come back into play.

I'll never forget an attorney friend I had years ago who was one of the funniest people I have ever met. He taught me a lot about laughing that I will never forget. The main thing he did to make things funny was that he would just take the every day things that were happening and turn them slightly sideways to a new angle of perception, and they honestly became hysterically funny. One day he and I were getting ready for a party and we were cutting up strawberries and he looked over at me and said, "What on earth do you do with these anyway—just cut on the dotted line?" Maybe you had to be there, but thinking about cutting up strawberries on the dotted line just really struck me as funny!

You can always watch funny shows or funny movies to get your "funny bone" working. Norman Cousins wrote a book years ago about how he took himself out of the hospital when he had been diagnosed with a life-threatening illness, and rented a motel room instead, and spent all his time watching funny movies. He watched funny movies all day long every day until he got better. He literally laughed himself back to health, much to his doctor's surprise.

Another way to develop your sense of humor and your lightheartedness is to find things to do just for the fun of it. Why not put aside making money or being responsible for a little while, and just think about what's fun for you? What has made you laugh and have fun in the past? I'm not talking about doing drugs or alcohol; I'm talking about having clean, good old-fashioned fun.

Maybe it would be playing charades with your family, or going sledding, or maybe planning a costume party. It doesn't have to be Halloween to do costumes; you could have a 'Ship-Wrecked Party' and invite your friends, or even a 'Hawaiian Luau!' Just changing the scenery or the props you're using usually gets people laughing when you're in a group.

Something that can be particularly funny is just learning to laugh at your own growth process. Some of the things that seemed totally overwhelming and insurmountable when you were facing them head-on can become very funny way when you finally get past them. They can become the best material for joking that you'll ever find. Those experiences can be absolutely hilarious when you learn to see the funny side of things.

You can also laugh and have fun with the people you love at the very things that you were arguing about just a few minutes ago. It's hard to believe till you experience it, but when you learn to detach yourself from the drama of it all, laughing at how ridiculous it is just becomes natural and easy and also very funny.

One of the most fun, rewarding things to do with laughter is to be the person who puts a smile on other people's faces. We all run into people who are hurting or struggling every day. One of the best gifts we can offer the people in our lives is to say something funny that helps them loosen up, and let go, and see the funny side of life. One of the quickest, easiest ways to make friends is to make other people laugh. Of course the gift we give through laughter comes back to us very quickly, because when we make them laugh, we're laughing too!

Laughter is often not really taken seriously by most of us on the spiritual path, yet many of the great teachers of our times say that hilarious, side-busting laughter is actually a sacred gift. They say that frequent, spontaneous, infectious laughter could be one of the important hallmarks of the truly enlightened being.

If you remember reading Carlos Castaneda's books, for example, Don Juan and his spiritual teacher Don Genaro are constantly having fits of laughter to the point where they fall on the ground and roll around laughing. Obviously Don Genero had a great sense of humor. Some of the other spiritual teachers even use laughter itself as a meditation. They teach people just to laugh for the joy of laughing, because laughter, in and of itself, raises our spiritual vibration.

Laughter stimulates physical healing and enhances our creativity. It rejuvenates our bodies. We release a large amount of physical and emotional tension when we laugh. Laughter improves our immune system. It relieves our stress and discharges our negative feelings. Laughter can also be very healing for our relationships because it opens our hearts. Laughter allows us to see the difficulties in our lives from a more transcendent, higher consciousness perspective.

Having a good sense of humor actually enables us to process information in a different way. Humor involves the entire brain and it actually serves to integrate and balance both hemispheres of our brains. The new perceptions we get when we laugh can often lead to finding healthier solutions to our problems and challenges. Learning to laugh regularly helps us learn to take ourselves less seriously. It supports us to develop a healthier, happier attitude and to invite more positive emotions into our lives.

I received a cute e-mail recently. It was an invitation to an "Over-Serious Anonymous 12-Step Program." The first couple steps of the 12-Step process were much like the AA program. It starts by admitting that we are powerless over our own seriousness and that because of this our lives have become unmanageable. It goes on to say that we have come to believe that only by lightening up could we achieve a state of health and non-seriousness. How very true! But I think we could take it a step further. I believe that it's only by lightening up that we can become the enlightened higher-consciousness beings we want to be. I personally believe that lightheartedness is the quickest and most delightful path to higher consciousness.

Nothing feels as good as some good, old-fashioned, gut-level laughter. *One thing you do want to be careful about, however, is never, never to laugh at another person's expense.* Laughing at someone else's pain is not funny, and it doesn't make you or them feel good. If you're teasing someone who knows you love them, and they know that it's a joke, that's okay, but be sure they think it's funny too.

So the homework today is going to be lighthearted and fun. Are you surprised? Go find your journal and lets get to work, okay? Ooops! I should have said let's start playing! You and I have worked long and hard to get to today's homework. I can hardly wait to reap the benefits, can you?

Homework Assignment: Chapter Sixteen

1. Before we get started, check in with yourself to see if there are any difficult feelings you need to work through today before you do this homework. If so, please go back to the homework in Chapter Three and work through the feelings till you come to a place of peace inside.

2. Now ask yourself if you are still blaming yourself or anyone else for your life in any way, or expecting someone else to make you happy. If so, go back and do the forgiveness homework in Chapter Seven. *Blame and guilt will always keep you from true lightheartedness!*

3. Okay, now I'd like you to write about what you could do to get out of the rut in your life and do something new and different. What are some new activities you could do, or new books you could read, or new plans you could make that would change the scenery and help you learn to laugh again. Write a paragraph about what you plan to do differently in the next few weeks.

4. Please take a moment and imagine yourself laughing, like you used to laugh when you were a youngster. Imagine the fun and silliness that would come from that, and how good it would feel to let your hair down and really let go and have fun! Then write about how that felt. *Remember to take five minutes every day to imagine yourself laughing, until your life changes to the point where you are laughing regularly every day.*

5. Think of some friends you have who like to laugh, and write about how you could spend more time with them. Developing your relationship with people who like to laugh gives you the opportunity to use them as a role model in developing your own sense of humor.

6. Make a list of some funny movies that you'd like to watch. You can always go back to movies that have made you laugh before, but keep adding to them! Imagine that you are a movie producer, and think about a funny movie you would make. Add that movie to your list. *The more you laugh, the more you want to laugh. It's very contagious!*

7. Write about some activities you could do with family or friends that would be fun and silly. What games could you play or what parties could you plan that would get everyone laughing, and being silly, and just having fun? *Remember that hilarious, side-busting laughter is a sacred gift.*

8. Write about something in your life that was painful or challenging at the time, but later, when you thought of it differently, it became hilariously funny.

9. Write about something that happened to you while doing this 33-day journey that was difficult at the time and then looked funny after it was over and done. Remember that learning to laugh at your own growth process is often the best material you'll ever find for humor. *Just be careful not to laugh at anyone else's pain while they're still feeling it. It's not funny when you're still in the middle of the emotional soup!*

10. Write a few paragraphs about how you could be the person to put a smile on other people's faces. How could you develop your own sense of humor and share it with others to brighten their lives? Remember that the gift of laughter comes back to you quickly when you laugh together with your friends!

11. Now write a few pages about how you feel after doing today's homework. Was this fun for you?

Okay, once again, great job! You know, you really are a dear soul! I can feel it through the ethers! It takes a lot of courage and persistence to hang in there and do this process on your own. Maybe someday you and I will be laughing together at how you overcame those challenges. In the meantime, I'm so proud of you! Keep laughing! It only gets better from here.

Chapter Seventeen

Heal Yourself
and Heal the Planet!

LeRoy

LeRoy grew up in a small town in Texas. He had two older sisters. His parents were immigrants from Lebanon. LeRoy's father was very controlling but he had a good sense of humor. He was gone a lot during LeRoy's childhood, doing his dry goods business and playing at the domino halls. LeRoy grew up never feeling like he was good enough to please his dad.

LeRoy's mother loved him dearly but she, too, was quite controlling and she could also be very smothering. She was angry with his dad for not being there and she tried to get from LeRoy the love that she was never able to get from her husband. LeRoy withdrew into himself, trying to escape the emotional pain to find nurturing and safety inside.

LeRoy had a powerful spiritual experience when he was in college. He learned that he had reality and unreality reversed. Before that time, he thought reality was inner pain, depression, self-judgment, lack of confidence, fear of others, and always having a struggle to move forward. Through his experience he discovered that real life is joy, peace, love, power, perception, and being one with a tremendous flow of love, grace, and peace. LeRoy decided he wanted to live this powerful reality every day!

After that, LeRoy realized he had a lot of work to do on himself to get healthy emotionally. He attended hundreds of inner healing and self-development groups and workshops to heal himself. He also became interested in helping others grow, so he went on to learn many self-development modalities. In his life career as an organizational consultant, he helped individuals and organizations become more emotionally integrated.

For a long time LeRoy thought that personal growth was a series of discovering his emotional blocks and then gaining an insight to overcome each block and moving to the next one. He felt like he was on an unending treadmill. He grew very tired of personal growth and for a time he felt angry with God.

Then in meditation one day he found himself on a beautiful hillside with sunshine and a nice breeze. He sensed Jesus coming to meet him. LeRoy heard Jesus say, "LeRoy, I love you. I am very happy that you are here. It's time for another level of learning and remembering for you. I would like you to choose to be born in an earth body. If you choose to be born, you will have a choice of these three sets of parents." Jesus went on to say, "Remember you don't have to do this. You can stay right here I love you unconditionally and the choice is all yours. If you choose to be born, you will not remember this conversation for a long time. Just remember, I am with you always!"

This meditation helped LeRoy realize that he is the only one responsible for all of his choices, all of his emotional blocks, and all of his life experiences. LeRoy laughs when he says that God was relieved to know he was no longer angry with him.

Within a short time, LeRoy was introduced to a new mind-body healing modality. This modality brought everything in his life together for him in a new and exciting way. LeRoy now has a goal to teach this healing modality to thousands of people while he's still here on the earth. He wants to help others to remember who they really are, be one with their true, shining spirit, and to live in their natural state of health and well-being.

Now at 73 years old, LeRoy is charming and delightful! He describes his life as very satisfying and gratifying. He has been married for 52 years and his marriage as better today than it has ever been. His clients regularly experience miracles from the exciting work he does with them and from the amazing skills they learn from his mind-body healing classes.

LeRoy recently wrote a new version of the epitaph he wants put on his grave when he's gone. It reads "I stumbled frequently. I got up and learned from it. From this I help people to loose their chains and to fly. I lived my life with joy!"

Day 33

Wow! We've been on quite a journey together, haven't we? It's starting to feel like we're old friends. I know for sure that if you've made it this far and done the homework I've prescribed, that your life will never, ever be the same. I'm so happy for you! I wish I could be there right now to give you a big hug and congratulate you for all your hard work and effort. You definitely deserve it!

Maybe you feel like it's too much information to put into practice all at once. Yes, I know, that's probably true. But that's why you have this trusty little book available to you. Take it with you and you've got it right there in your back pocket any time you need to pull it out and refer back to something you learned. Isn't that a fun idea? My clients often tell me about times when they were in a situation that was challenging to them and they think to themselves "What would Kari say about this?" and then the answer just comes to them and they do it. When they tell me about it, we have a good laugh!

You see, it's not actually about what I would say or do, it's connecting to your own spirit, and trusting that your own inner guidance will help you and show you how to face each new challenge in your life. But if I can represent that inner guidance to you for a short time in your life, I'm very happy to do that. As a matter of fact, I feel very honored to have that role.

I started this book after giving my last personal growth workshop six months ago. The workshops that my friends and I have given over the years are such incredible, high-consciousness, spiritual experiences that I wanted to find some way to share them with you. I know that there are beautiful souls like you all over the planet who may not have the same opportunity we have. So I've done my best through this book to offer you a similar opportunity to heal your own past and start your life fresh and new, with fresh, new energy and new enthusiasm to go out there and live what you've learned and make your life what you want it to be.

So, let me tell you what my personal hopes and dreams are for you, okay? More than anything in the world, I want you to have the chance to really live a life of love, joy and peace, because I know from my own experience how truly wonderful that can be. My personal life has gone from depression to happiness through doing my own personal growth. I'd love for you to know how that feels.

I also want you to live from your heart and express who you really are in your every day life. I want you to have deep, wonderful friendships with others who love and support you. I want you to have the experience of letting loose and laughing every day from deep inside yourself. I want you to have the joy of appreciating the sweet, special moments in life and really drinking in the beauty and wonder of each beautiful day. I want you to know depth, meaning, joy and fulfillment of giving to others and having it come back to you.

In short, I want you to be so blissfully happy that you want to tell others how wonderful you feel so they too will choose to do the emotional healing it takes to change their lives. Wouldn't it be incredible if we could start the ball rolling and other people picked up on it, until people all over the planet decided to live from love and joy and peace? That is my dream, to be a small part of a big shift on the planet that affects everyone's life for the better. Wouldn't you like to join me?

Did you know that each person who heals him or her self affects everyone else on the planet? It's true! Have you ever heard the story of the hundredth monkey? The story comes from a book called *The Hundredth Monkey*, by Ken Keyes Jr., and it's a story about monkeys on an island who decided to wash their coconuts before they ate them. First, one monkey decided to wash his coconut in the ocean before he ate it. Before long another monkey on the island saw what the first monkey was doing, and he got the idea, so he, too, washed his coconut in the ocean before he ate it. Soon more and more monkeys on the island joined them, until before long, all the monkeys on the island were washing their coconuts in the ocean before they ate them.

What was most interesting about this story was that the scientists who were observing this change of behavior discovered that when the whole island of monkeys began to wash their coconuts, the monkeys on another island nearby also started washing their coconuts. Monkeys obviously have no way to communicate island to island, so the scientists decided it had to be that the consciousness of the monkeys on the first island affected the consciousness of the monkeys on the second island.

The scientists deduced from this observation that our human consciousness is affected in the same way. When one of us tries something new that really works, someone else picks up on it and tries it too. If it works for them, the ball starts rolling till more and more people join in. Soon the consciousness of all the people who are doing the new behavior together affects the consciousness of other people all over the planet who are not even in contact with the people who originally started the change. Isn't that a fascinating thought?

The truth is that you and I together are already a part of the planetary consciousness that is changing. The change started happening in the 1960s when a few people started talking about love, peace and higher consciousness. If you look at how the world has changed since then, you'll see that we're already in a huge change that is taking place around us even as we speak. Think about the current awareness of issues like domestic violence, and verbal, physical and sexual abuse. Think of the awareness we now have of issues like self-esteem or higher consciousness. I'm sure you'll see what I'm referring to.

But even though our world is already changing, every soul that heals today still affects another soul, and another, and another. *Please remember that you are a very important part of the change that is happening.* When you open your heart and decide to live from love and peace, it will affect everyone you come in contact with.

When you laugh regularly and have fun every day, other people will want to know what changed in your life. When they see how it's working for you, some of them will ask you what you did, and some of them will decide to try it too. Then more people will choose to heal, and they, too, will affect the people in their lives, and the ripples will continue widening until they spread all over the globe. Isn't that fun to think about?

One of the joys of my work is watching how each person who heals emotionally affects hundreds and thousands of others in their life. It's fascinating to watch how the healing ripples out into more and more lives, and more and more work and business situations. I love hearing the stories of all the creative ways that people find to affect their families, their careers, and their communities. It's such an amazing process! I thank God regularly that I get to play a part in this incredible healing revolution all over the planet.

But each of us has to keep choosing growth and lightheartedness every day. No matter how far we get on the path of growth, life continues to offer us new challenges every day. We could always go back to the old ways, and live our lives from fear, and guilt and shame, and act out our emotional pain on innocent, unsuspecting people in our lives. Or we can choose to live from love, joy and peace, and treat people the way we want to be treated, and be a role model for others who are struggling to help them to make healthier choices in their lives.

When you choose to live from love, joy, and peace, and you choose to be an instrument of God's love and peace in the world, the Universe supports you. Your life becomes filled with loving, supportive people. Your dreams and desires manifest more quickly. Your self-esteem grows in leaps and bounds because there is so much love coming back to you all the time. You see, the energy you give out really does come back to you!

So it all comes back to you and to you deciding which choices you want to make every day. What do you want more than anything in the world? Do you want to live from love, joy and peace and be a part of this exciting change that's happening? Great! I'm so happy that you are making that choice! My dream for you is that you will choose every day to open your heart and live from love.

My dream is that you will affect hundreds and thousands of people you come in contact with over the next fifty years of your life. My dream for you is that you will give out so much love that your life will start to feel like it's charmed when all that love you've given comes back to you. My dream for you is that you will get to experience the unbelievable happiness that comes from living each day from love, joy and peace.

I have another very important dream I want to share with you today. I have a dream that you and I together, along with everyone else who is choosing to live from love, peace and lightheartedness in the world, could actually find a way to effect some of the major world issues in our lifetime. Wouldn't it be incredible if we, together, could find a way to heal the environment and treat our beautiful earth with love and respect, the way she has treated us?

Wouldn't it also be amazing if we could find a way to end world hunger, so that there wouldn't be children starving to death anywhere on our planet? Wouldn't it be great if our world leaders could learn about love, peace and harmony and work together to create peace and harmony between nations?

Remember the story of the hundredth monkey. If enough of us change our lives, and change our ways of thinking, and change the way we treat each other, eventually our world consciousness will also be affected. Our leaders will have no choice but to learn to open up their own hearts and work together in love and harmony and peace.

I have tears in my eyes as I complete this. It's been great getting to know you! I'm going to miss working with you. I hope someday you and I will meet in person. If not, our souls will always know each other in spirit. Our hearts will share the joy of living from love, joy, peace and higher consciousness and being a part of this incredible planetary shift!

Homework Assignment: Chapter Seventeen

1. Go back and read over all your homework assignments in this 33-day process. Look at the amazing progress you've made!

2. Write a thank-you letter to yourself for all your hard work and effort! *Don't skip this one! If you want to keep growing, you have to remember to appreciate yourself for the work and effort you are putting into it.*

3. If you are willing, I'd love to have you write an e-mail to me at Kari@kari-joys.com answering the following questions:
    1. Please tell me about yourself, your age, your gender, your occupation, the city you live in, whether you are a teenager, a mom or dad, a grandmother or grandfather, or anything else you're willing to share.
    2. What were the original issues, symptoms, or problems that you were seeking help for?
    3. What were your original fears about doing this process? For example, were you afraid that nothing would help, or that your situation was too serious, or maybe that it had gone on too long to be helped in 33 days by a simple little book? Please specify for me what your fears or concerns were when you started.
    4. How have your symptoms changed since you started this journey?
    5. What have you learned about yourself from this 33-day journey?
    6. How has your life changed as a result of your new attitude and awareness?
    7. What do you plan to do differently in the future, now that you have these new tools to utilize?
    8. What did you appreciate about my book?
    9. What do you think I could do to improve this book to make it more helpful to others in the future?
    10. Is it okay to use what you've written as a testimonial on my website or in a future book to help others believe that they, too, can heal? Would you prefer that I use a different first name?

4. Now write a few pages in your own journal about how you feel after
    doing today's homework.

I want to thank you from the bottom of my heart for giving me this
opportunity to be a part of your life. It's been a real joy working with you.
I know that God will bless you on your journey as he has blessed me on mine!
Love and de-light, Kari

Bibliography

Adam, *DreamHealer 2, Guide to Self-Empowerment,* (DreamHealer, 2004, Canada)

Anderson, Susan, *The Journey from Abandonment to Healing,* (Berkley Books, 2000, New York, New York)

Bass, Ellen, and Davis, Laura, *The Courage to Heal* (Harper and Roe Publishers, 1988, New York, New York)

Bays, Brandon, *The Journey, A Road Map to the Soul* (Simon and Schuster, 1999, New York, NY)

Beattie, Melodie, *Codependent No More; How to Stop Controlling Others and Start Caring for Yourself* (Harper and Row Publishers, 1987, New York, NY)

Bradshaw, John, *Homecoming: Reclaiming and Championing Your Inner Child (Bantam Books, 1990, New York, NY)*

Bradshaw, John, *Healing the Shame that Binds You* (Health Communications, 1988, Deerfield Beach Florida)

Bradshaw, John, *The Family, A Revolutionary Way of Self Discovery* (Health Communications, 1988, Deerfield Beach, Florida)

Cameron, Julia, *The Artist's Way, A Spiritual Path to Higher Creativity* (Putnam Publishing, 1992, New York, NY)

Canfield, Jack, *The Success Principles; How to Get From Where You Are to Where You Want to Be* (HarperCollins Books, 2005, New York, NY)

Castenada, Carlos, *The Teachings of Don Juan, A Yaqui Way of Knowledge* (Simon and Schuster, Inc., 1968, New York, NY)

Cousins, Norman, *Anatomy of an Illness as Perceived by the Patient: Reflections on Healing and Regeneration* (Bantam Books, 1979, New York, NY)

Daniel, Alma, and Wyllie, Timothy, and Ramer, Andrew, *Ask Your Angels: A Practical Guide to Working with the Messengers of Heaven to Empower and Enrich Your Life* (Ballantine Books, 1992, New York, NY)

Das, Lama Surya, *Awakening the Buddha Within; Tibetan Wisdom for the Western World* (Broadway Books, 1997, New York, NY)

Dass, Ram, and Bush, Mirabai, *Compassion in Action; Setting Out on the Path of Service* (Bell Tower, 1992, New York, NY)

Dossey, MD, Larry, *Prayer is Good Medicine* (Harper Collins Publishing, 1996, New York, NY)

Engel, Beverly, *The Emotionally Abusive Relationship, How to Stop Being Abused and How to Stop Abusing* (John Wiley and Sons, Inc., 2002, Hoboken, NJ)

Evans, Patricia, *The Verbally Abusive Relationship, How to Recognize It and How to Respond* (Bob Adams Inc., 1992, Holbrook, MA)

Farmer, MA, Steven, *Adult Children of Abusive Parents*, (Ballantine Books, 1989, New York, NY)

Ford Debbie *The Best Year of Your Life: Dream It, Plan It, Live It* (Harper Collins, 2005, New York, NY)

Forward, Susan, *Toxic Parents, Overcoming Their Hurtful Legacy and Reclaiming Your Life* (Bantam Books, 1989, New York, New York)

Gawain, Shakti, *Creative Visualization* (Whatever Publishing, 1978, Mill Valley, CA)

Glover, Ph.D., Wes A., *No More Mr. Nice Guy, A Proven Plan For Getting What You Want in Love, Sex and Life* (Running Press Book Publishers, 2000, Philadelphia, PA)

Gossett, Susan Ann, *An Angel's Guide to Heaven on Earth* (Angelic Mission Publishing, 1992, Portland, OR)

Grabhorn, Lynn, *Excuse Me, Your Life Is Waiting, The Astonishing Power of Feelings* (Hampton Roads Publishing, 2000, Charlottesville, VA)

Hay Louise *I Can Do It: How to Use Affirmations to Change Your Life (Hay House, 2004, Carlsbad, CA)*

Hay, Louise, *You Can Heal Your Life* (Hay House, 1984, Santa Monica, CA)

Hay, Louise, *101 Power Thoughts (Hay House, 2004, Carlsbad, CA)*

Hendricks Ph.D., Gay, *Learning to Love Yourself Workbook* (Simon and Schuster, Inc, 1990, New York, NY)

Hicks, Esther and Jerry, *Ask and It Is Given, Learning to Manifest Your Desires* (Hay House, 2004, Carlsbad, CA)

Jampolsky, MD, Jerald, *Love is Letting Go of Fear* (Bantam Books, 1970, New York, NY)

Jeffers, Ph.D., Susan, *Feel the Fear and Do It Anyway: Dynamic Techniques for Turning Fear, Indecision and Anger into Power, Action and Love* (Ballantine Books, 1987, New York, NY)

Kabat-Zinn, Jon, *Wherever You Go, There You Are; Mindfulness Meditation in Everyday Life* (Hyperion, 1994, New York, NY)

Keyes Jr., Ken, *The Hundredth Monkey* (Love Line Books, 1981, Living Love Center)

Lew, Mike, *Victims No Longer, The Classic Guide for Men Recovering from Sexual Child Abuse* (Harper Collins, 2004, New York, NY)

Limmer, Eleanor, *Balance, Beyond Illness to Health and Wholeness* (Freedom Press, 2002, Spokane, WA)

Luthman, Shirley Gehrke, *Energy And Personal Power* (Mehetabel & Company, 1982, San Rafael, CA)

Marooney, Kimberly, *Angel Blessings; Cards of Sacred Guidance and Inspiration* (Fair Winds Press, 1995, Gloucester, MA)

Melchizedeck, Drunvello, *Spirit of Ma'at, Online Community and Webzine* (*http://www.spiritofmaat.com*)

Myss, Caroline, *Anatomy of the Spirit, the Seven Stages of Power and Healing* (Crown Publishers, 1996, New York, NY)

Myss, Caroline, *Why People Don't Heal And How They Can* (Random House, 1997, New York, NY)

Mueller, Wayne, *Legacy of the Heart, The Spiritual Advantages of a Painful Childhood* (Simon and Schuster, 1992, New York, NY)

Morton, Andrew, *Diana, Her True Story (Simon and Schuster, 1992, New York, NY)*

Norwood, Robin, *Women Who Love Too Much; When You Keep Wishing and Hoping He'll Change* (Pocket Books, 1985, New York, NY)

Peck, MD, M. Scott, *The Road Less Traveled.* (Simon and Schuster, 1978, New York, NY)

Pert, Ph.D., Candace, *Molecules of Emotion, The Science Behind Mind-Body Medicine* (Scribner, 1997, New York, NY)

Real, Terrance, *I Don't Want To Talk About It; Overcoming the Secret Legacy of Male Depression* (Simon and Schuster, 1997, New York, NY)

Redfield, James, *The Celestine Prophecy, An Adventure* (Satori Publishing, 1993, Hoover, Alabama)

Rosenberg, Ph.D., Marshall B., *Non-Violent Communication, A Language of Compassion* (Puddledancer Press, 1999, Del Mar, CA)

Roth, Ph.D., Ron, *Holy Spirit for Healing: Merging Ancient Wisdom With Modern Medicine* (Hay House, 2001, Carlsbad, CA)

Roth, Ph.D., Ron, *Reclaim Your Spiritual Power* (Hay House, 2002, Carlsbad, CA)

Sarno, MD, John E., *The Mind-Body Prescription, Healing the Body, Healing the Pain* (Warner Books, 1998, New York, NY)

Seligman, Martin, E. P., *Learned Optimism, How to Change Your Mind and Change Your Life* (Simon and Schuster, 1990, New York, NY)

Tipping, Colin C., *Radical Forgiveness, Making Room for the Miracle* (Global 13 Publications, 1997, Marietta, GA)

Tolle, Eckart, *The Power of Now; A Guide To Spiritual Enlightenment* (New World Library, 1999, Novato, CA)

Virtue, Ph.D., Doreen, *Archangel Oracle Cards, A 45-Card Deck and Guidebook* (Hay House, 2004, Carlsbad, CA)

Virtue, Ph.D., Doreen, *Archangels and Ascended Masters; A Guide To Working and Healing With Divinities and Deities* (Hay House, 2003, Carlsbad, CA)

Virtue, Ph.D., Doreen, *Divine Guidance: How to Have A Dialogue With God and Your Guardian Angels* (Renaissance Books, 1998, New York)

Virtue, Ph.D., Doreen, *Healing With The Angels; How the Angels Can Assist in Every Area of Your Life* (Hay House, Inc., 1999, Carlsbad, CA)

Walsch, Neale Donald, *Conversations with God, an Uncommon Dialogue* (Hampton Roads Publishing Company, 1995, Charlottesville, VA)

Weiss, MD, Brian, *Messages From The Masters; Tapping In To The Power Of Love* (Warner Books, 2000, New York, NY)

Whitfield M.D., Charles, *Healing the Child Within* (Health Communications Inc., 1989, Deerfield Beach, Florida)

Williamson, Marianne, *Illuminata; Thoughts, Prayers, Rights of Passage* (Random House, Inc., 1994, New York, New York)

Williamson, Marianne, *Return to Love; Reflections on the Principles of "A Course in Miracles"* (HarperCollins, 1992, New York, New York)

Yogananda, Paramahansa, *Autobiography of a Yogi* (Self Realization Fellowship, 1946, Los Angeles, CA)

Yuen, Kam, *Instant Pain Elimination; How to stop the pain you feel in two minutes or less* (CEM Publishers, 2003, Canoga Park, California)

Zukav, Gary, *The Seat of the Soul* (Simon and Schuster, 1989, New York, NY)

Sign up for Kari Joys' free monthly newsletter online!

As you know, having patience and persistence with your emotional healing can sometimes be a challenge. Receiving Kari's delightful monthly newsletter will help you to remember your true shining spirit! It will also let you know of Kari's new books and CDs that are coming available and it will notify you of her exciting upcoming events. Go to Kari's website at www.kari-joys.com to sign up today!

Facilitate an Emotional Healing Journey support group!

If you enjoyed *Choosing Light-Heartedness* and found it helpful yourself, why not start a support group in your area for emotional healing? Remember that having loving support in your life is what helps you stay patient and persistent on your own emotional healing journey.

Kari has provided a free instructor's manual on her website at www.kari-joys.com that allows you to guide an emotional healing support group utilizing one chapter from her book each week. You can also check Kari's website to get a discount for ten, twenty-five, fifty, or one hundred books.

Whatever you do, we sincerely hope that you will share the joy and lightheartedness you've received from Kari's delightful book with as many people in your life as possible!

Please visualize with us!

We are planning to create a Higher Consciousness Mind-Body Healing Center in the Spokane, Washington area with the proceeds from this book. We'd love to have you visualize it with us! Just imagine the Healing Center already completed and operating smoothly and efficiently.

Imagine the Healing Center being out in a beautiful natural area where we can feel close to God and the angels. Imagine the compassionate staff at the Higher Consciousness Mind-Body Healing Center helping thousands of people to heal physically, emotionally and spiritually. When the Healing Center has manifested on the physical plane, you'll be able to visit us and enjoy a lovely, relaxing atmosphere for your own personal growth.